Mic

CW00421773

4.0

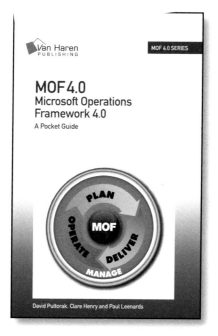

Van Haren
PUBLISHING

MOF 4.0
Microsoft Operations Framework 4.0
A Pocket Guide

PLAN

MOF

OPERATE

DELIVER

MANAGE

David Pultorak, Clare Henry and Paul Leenards

MOF 4.0

Microsoft Operations Framework 4.0
A Pocket Guide

Colofon

Title:	Microsoft Operations Framework (MOF) 4.0
Authors:	David Pultorak (Lead Author), Clare Henry, and Paul Leenards
Publisher:	Van Haren Publishing, Zaltbommel, www.vanharen.net
ISBN:	978 90 8753 286 4
Print:	First edition, first impression, September 2008
Layout and design:	CO2 Premedia, Amersfoort-NL
Cover design:	O2, Norwich, UK
Copyright:	Van Haren Publishing

MOF 4.0 is Copyright © 2008 Microsoft Corporation. The Microsoft Operations Framework 4.0 is provided with permission from Microsoft Corporation. Microsoft, Exchange Server, SQL Server, and Windows Server are either registered trademarks or trademarks of Microsoft Corporation in the United States and/or other countries.

For any further enquiries about Van Haren Publishing, please send an e-mail to: info@vanharen.net

Authors:

Dave Pultorak (Pultorak & Associates, Ltd.), Clare Henry (Microsoft Corporation), and Paul Leenards (Getronics Consulting)

Contributors:

Jerry Dyer (Senior Program Manager, Microsoft Corporation)

Don Lemmex (Senior Program Manager, Microsoft Corporation)

Betsy Norton-Middaugh (Senior Program Manager, Microsoft Corporation)

Jason Osborne (Program Manager, Microsoft Corporation)

Reviewers:

Tom Bondi (Architect, Operations Consulting, Microsoft Corporation)

Rob van der Burg (Operations Consulting Manager, Microsoft Corporation)

Edwin Griffioen (Operations Consultant, Microsoft Corporation)

Khalid Hakim (Operations Consultant, Microsoft Corporation)

Lasse Wilén Kristensen (Senior Consultant, Microsoft Corporation)

Shawn LaBelle (Architect, Operations Consulting, Microsoft Corporation)

Aidan Lawes (ITIL expert, ex-CEO of itSMF UK)

Steve McReynolds (Senior Consultant MCS, Microsoft Corporation)

Niel Nickolaisen (CIO, Headwaters Incorporated)

Michael Polzin (Operations Consultant, Microsoft Corporation)

Anders Ravnholt (System Center Consultant, Microsoft Corporation)

Gary Roos (Senior Operations Consultant, Microsoft Corporation)

Stephanie Saad (Group Manager, VSTS, Microsoft Corporation)

Gokula Thilagar (SDET, VSTS, Microsoft Corporation)

Zheng Tu (SDET, VSTS, Microsoft Corporation)

Contents

Foreword

Successful IT requires knowledge and process—not just products and technologies. And providing this guidance is a growing concern: just look at the abundance of service management frameworks available for a variety of industries.

The big bet with IT management frameworks is that relatively small changes in thinking and acting on the part of IT professionals will bring about large improvements in costs, productivity, customer and employee satisfaction, and the availability and reliability of IT services.

With MOF 4.0, Microsoft takes up this big bet. This pocket guide presents MOF 4.0 in capsule form.

Just for a moment, think of a management framework as you would a vitamin supplement. As anyone who's ever had a cold knows, it's never enough to just offer the pill itself; timing, dosage, and mode of delivery have a lot to do with whether you stay well or get sick. Well, it's the same with IT service management guidance: it's not enough to get the content right. Getting through to overworked, distracted IT pros—really getting them to think and act differently—requires getting the "dosage" and delivery method right. So what does "right" look like? It's...

> **...relevant.** It speaks to real IT pros in real roles, about problems that are of current concern to them, that affect their day-to-day activities and deliverables.

> **...practical.** It is actually useful in solving problems and pursuing opportunities in a meaningful and directed way. It's at the right "zoom level" to be useful—you don't need a

map of the universe if you're just trying to find the grocery store.

...concise. It quickly gets to the point—IT pros have zero time to waste.

...structured and extendable. It's organized in a manner that is easily navigable, with links to further guidance, services, products, and solutions.

...outcome-focused. It concentrates on key results, and provides ideas for getting there, with room for multiple paths to the same end. Guidance that focuses on activities without a clear vision or tie to their intended business results is theoretical, not practical.

...community-driven. It's been created and enhanced by, and for, like-minded IT professionals. It's open and free to use, and there are plenty of opportunities to contribute back.

MOF 4.0 was designed to get IT service management guidance right. It's refreshing to me to see a framework that recognizes the vital importance of IT pros and places them back in the middle of the action. I'm excited to discover a form factor right for making a real difference in their performance, and in the end in the performance of the IT services they plan, deliver, operate, and manage. And I'm delighted to see the soul of the service management movement in evidence in the MOF 4.0 community website. Microsoft recognizes that customers and partners have developed great ideas and best practices, and these have been reflected in the development of MOF 4.0. I applaud Microsoft for its forward thinking, and I encourage you not only to use this book, but to contribute to the MOF community and benefit from the contribution of others.

David Pultorak
Founder and Chairman
Pultorak & Associates, Ltd.

1. MOF 4.0 Overview and FAQ

Introduction to MOF 4.0

First released in 1999, Microsoft® Operations Framework (MOF) is Microsoft's structured approach to helping its customers achieve operational excellence across the entire IT service lifecycle. Microsoft is known for offering enterprise-class server platforms and products, including Windows Server®, Exchange Server® and SQL Server®, but technology alone isn't enough—to meet the tough challenges facing IT, organizations increasingly require guidance structured within a management framework. MOF was originally created to give IT professionals the knowledge and processes required to align their work in managing these platforms cost-effectively and to achieve high reliability, availability, and security. Microsoft created MOF to provide this guidance.

Since the first version of MOF was written, demands on IT have changed. Organizations are now faced with

- Increasing IT's business value.
- Responding to regulatory requirements.
- Increased demand to do more with less.

This newest version, MOF 4.0, was built to respond to these challenges.

Goal of MOF 4.0

The guidance in MOF is intended to help organizations create, operate, and support IT services while ensuring that the investment in IT delivers expected business value at an acceptable level of risk.

Using MOF can help organizations create an environment where IT and the business work together toward operational maturity—MOF 4.0 provides a proactive model that defines processes and standard procedures to promote efficiency and effectiveness. It gives organizations a logical approach to decision-making and to the planning, deployment, and support of IT services.

MOF 4.0 Frequently Asked Questions

What is new in MOF 4.0?

The guidance in MOF 4.0 has been structured for the IT pro. Often, the downside to using a management framework is the "knowing/ doing gap"—the difficulty in equating abstract theories with the day-to-day activities IT pros perform. To address this, MOF 4.0 introduces a new structure for its service management functions (SMFs)—one that emphasizes outcomes, results, and roles in a format that's easy to reference.

In addition, MOF 4.0 has been expanded and enhanced to:
- Reflect a single, comprehensive IT lifecycle.
- Integrate best practices from Microsoft Solutions Framework (MSF).
- Create clear accountabilities.
- Align IT with business needs and goals.
- Address governance, risk, policy, and compliance.

- Support ISO/IEC 20000, CoBiT and ITIL V3.
- Enhance continuous improvement through community involvement.

For reference on how MOF 4.0 has changed, you can refer to the MOF 3.0 – MOF 4.0 Comparison chart located at the end of this Pocket Guide.

How much effort will it take to implement MOF 4.0?

Your goal should be to solve problems and promote efficiency in your organization, not to "implement" MOF. You can use MOF to drive key decisions, create and manage key policies and risks, clearly define roles and accountabilities, and define and enact processes for your organization—all in an efficient and practical manner. Because the scope of any problem or opportunity will determine the amount of effort required, MOF 4.0 has been designed to help overburdened IT professionals quickly access useful, relevant content. It contains practical guidance for everyday tasks and activities—not just theory—to efficiently and effectively address those problems. Its streamlined approach makes it possible for users to either implement the entire framework or simply use one component of the framework to solve a particular problem.

How is MOF 4.0 structured, and why?

The guidance in MOF consists of a series of phase overviews and SMFs. These describe the activities necessary for successful IT service management—from the assessment that launches a new or improved service, through the process of optimizing an existing service, all the way to the retirement of an outdated service.

The guidance has been written to meet the needs of three audiences: Corporate Information Officers (CIOs), IT managers, and IT professionals.

- Overview guides are directed toward CIOs, who need to see the big picture.
- Overview and workflow information in function-specific guides is geared toward IT managers who need to understand IT service strategies.
- Activities in function-specific guides are meant for the IT professionals who implement MOF in their day-to-day activities.

How does the content structure support ease of use and practical application?
The SMFs are anchored by pertinent questions, inputs, outputs, and best practices for each activity, and tables provide a format that's concise and easy to follow. The questions help drive decisions that are relevant for your organization. By answering the questions, you help determine where to focus (or not), which supports organizational maturation.

How does MOF address governance, risk, and compliance?
Governance, risk, and compliance are addressed in the Manage Layer, which is the foundation for the phases (Plan, Deliver, and Operate). Governance identifies the decision makers and stakeholders, determines accountability for actions and responsibilities for outcomes, and addresses how expected performance will be evaluated. Risk management occurs throughout the entire IT lifecycle as well; it addresses business decisions, policy adherence, application development, and operational procedures. Risk also determines what business controls need to be in place. Compliance guides behavior throughout the lifecycle to ensure that governance and risk management activities are addressed. The management reviews in each phase show how IT is performing against corporate governance, risk, and compliance objectives.

How can I learn more and share ideas?

A central component of MOF 4.0 is its online community—a place where IT professionals can share service management knowledge and best practices, communicating both with each other and with Microsoft. MOF 4.0 provides a platform that integrates contribution sharing, blogs, forums, online training, and feedback to support the community and keep it ahead of ever-shifting IT trends. To visit MOF online, go to www.microsoft.com/mof.

Will MOF 4.0 work with the framework I'm currently using?

MOF 4.0 is backward-compatible with all previous versions of MOF, and can easily integrate policies, tasks, or activities based on other frameworks. MOF 4.0 was designed to provide you with a clear picture of how the entire IT lifecycle is interrelated, what decisions are required, and what outcomes are vital, yet leaves it up to the IT organization to determine the areas of focus. An organization or IT professional can use all of MOF 4.0 or just one component of the framework to solve a particular problem.

Does MOF 4.0 align with other IT frameworks?

MOF 4.0 aligns with ISO/IEC 20000, ITIL, and CoBiT, which are well-known service management tools. Guidance that takes a theoretical, high-level approach often leaves the reader at a loss about its application; MOF 4.0 contains fundamental IT service management guidance, but takes a more streamlined approach to meet the needs of the IT pro.

ITIL®

There are many similarities between MOF and ITIL®. ITIL® V3 defines the top-level processes and functions that constitute best practices in IT management and the service lifecycle. ITIL® V3 is a vast compendium of information that addresses the breadth of IT activities throughout its more than 1300 pages of concepts and models. MOF streamlines the IT service lifecycle approach by using common terms and delivering the guidance in a concise and meaningful way.

CoBiT

CoBiT is an auditing tool developed by industry professionals responsible for ensuring that organizations are meeting certain regulatory requirements. CoBiT addresses policies from regulatory bodies such as the Securities and Exchange Commission (SEC), the European Union (EU), the Health Insurance Portability and Accountability Act (HIPAA), the Data Protection Act, Basel I/II, and Sarbanes Oxley (SOX). MOF identifies the accepted set of controls for IT professionals who have to implement, execute, follow, or report IT policies and navigate risks every day. MOF 4.0 includes policy creation in the Plan Phase as well as support for IT governance, risk management, and compliance throughout the entire IT service lifecycle. Risk management and internal controls provide a coherent focus throughout the lifecycle and demonstrate the interconnectedness of all IT activities.

ISO/IEC 20000

ISO/IEC 20000 is an IT service management process standard created by the International Organization for Standardization. To receive ISO certification, businesses must meet certain goals and objectives set forth by the organization. MOF 4.0 identifies clear outcomes and measures for each process within the IT service lifecycle; its guidance helps businesses streamline their decision making and identify best practices for effective service management.

Figure 1-1 shows the relationship between MOF and other industry standards, as well as how Microsoft uses community input and best practices to align its solution and platform strategy to support these standards.

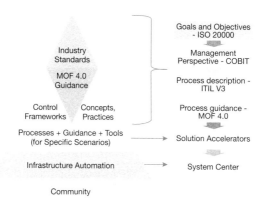

Figure 1-1. The relationship between MOF and other industry standards

2. MOF 4.0 at a Glance

How MOF 4.0 is Structured

The guidance in MOF 4.0 consists of a series of phase overviews and service management function (SMF) guides. These describe the activities that need to occur for successful IT service management — from the assessment that launches a new or improved service, through the process of optimizing an existing service, all the way to the retirement of an outdated service.

The guidance is written for a number of audiences — Chief Information Officers (CIOs), IT managers, and IT professionals:

- Overview guides are directed toward CIOs, who need to see the big picture.
- Overview and workflow information in function-specific guides is geared toward IT managers, who need to understand the IT service strategies.
- Activities in function-specific guides are meant for the IT professionals, who implement MOF within their work.

The MOF 4.0 guidance is available on Microsoft TechNet at http://www.microsoft.com/technet/solutionaccelerators/cits/mo/mof/default.mspx.

The IT Service Lifecycle

The IT service lifecycle describes the life of an IT service, from planning and optimizing the IT service to align with the business strategy, through the design and delivery of the IT service, to its ongoing operation and support. Underlying all of this is a foundation of IT governance, risk management, compliance, team organization, and change management.

The Lifecycle Phases

The IT service lifecycle is composed of three ongoing phases and one foundational layer that operates throughout all of the other phases. They are:

- The Plan Phase.
- The Deliver Phase.
- The Operate Phase.
- The Manage Layer.

Figure 2-1. The IT service lifecycle

Your IT organization is probably managing many services at any given time, and these services may be in different phases of the IT service lifecycle. Therefore, you will get the most benefit from

MOF if you have a basic understanding about how all phases of the lifecycle operate and how they work together.

- The Plan Phase is generally the preliminary phase. The goal of this phase is to plan and optimize an IT service strategy in order to support business goals and objectives.
- The Deliver Phase comes next. The goal of this phase is to ensure that IT services are developed effectively, are deployed successfully, and are ready for Operations.
- Next is the Operate Phase. The goal of this phase is to ensure that IT services are operated, maintained, and supported in a way that meets business needs and expectations.
- The Manage Layer is the foundation of the IT service lifecycle. Its goal is to provide operating principles and best practices to ensure that the investment in IT delivers expected business value at an acceptable level of risk. This phase is concerned with IT governance, risk, compliance, roles and responsibilities, change management, and configuration. Processes in this phase take place during all phases of the lifecycle.

Following the guidelines contained in MOF 4.0 can help:

- Decrease risks through better coordination between teams.
- Recognize compliance implications when policies are reviewed.
- Anticipate and mitigate reliability impacts.
- Discover possible integration issues prior to production.
- Prevent performance issues by anticipating thresholds.
- Effectively adapt to new business needs.

Service Management Functions within the Phases

Each phase of the IT service lifecycle contains service management functions (SMFs) that define and structure the processes, people, and activities required to align IT services to the requirements of the business. The SMFs are grouped together in phases that mirror the IT service lifecycle. Each SMF is anchored within a lifecycle phase and contains a unique set of goals and outcomes supporting the objectives of that phase. An IT service's readiness to move from one phase to the next is confirmed by management reviews (MRs), which ensure that goals are being achieved in an appropriate fashion and that IT's goals are aligned with the goals of the organization.

Figure 2-2 shows the IT service lifecycle phases, the SMFs, and the management reviews within each phase.

Figure 2-2. The IT service lifecycle phases and SMFs

Although each SMF can be thought of as a stand-alone set of processes, it is important to understand how the SMFs in all of the phases work to ensure that service delivery is at the desired quality and risk level. In some phases (such as Deliver), the SMFs are performed sequentially, while in other phases (such as Operate), the SMFs may be performed simultaneously to create the outputs for the phase.

Management Reviews (MRs)

For each phase in the lifecycle, MRs serve to bring together information and people to determine the status of IT services and to establish readiness to move forward in the lifecycle. MRs are internal controls that provide management validation checks, ensuring that goals are being achieved in an appropriate fashion, and that business value is considered throughout the IT service lifecycle. The goals of management reviews, no matter where they happen in the lifecycle, are straightforward:

- Provide management oversight and guidance.
- Act as internal controls at the phase level of the IT lifecycle.
- Assess the state of activities and prevent premature advancement into the next phases.
- Capture organizational learning.
- Improve processes.

The MRs, their locations in the IT service lifecycle, and their inputs and outputs are shown in the following table.

Table 2-1. MOF Management Reviews

MR	Owned by Phase	Inputs	Outputs
Service Alignment	Plan	• Results of the Operational Health Review • Service Level Agreements (SLA) • Customer input	• Opportunity for a new or improved project • Request for changes to SLA
Portfolio	Plan	• Project proposals	• Formation of a team • Initial project charter
Project Plan Approved	Deliver	• Business requirements • Vision statement	• Formation of the project team • Approved project plan
Release Readiness	Deliver	• Documentation showing that the release meets requirements • Documentation showing that the release is stable • Documentation showing that the release is ready for operations	• Go/no go decision about release
Operational Health	Operate	• Operating level agreement (OLA) documents • OLA performance reports • Operational guides and service-solution specifications	• Request for changes to the OLA documents • Request for changes to the IT services • Configuration changes to underlying technology components

The Elements of SMFs

The content architecture in MOF 4.0 is designed so that an organization can quickly and efficiently apply the concepts, best practices and ideas to their organization. You can use a "start anywhere, go everywhere" approach—simply choose a particular outcome, role, goal, or process as a starting point. Each of these elements is an interrelated part of a whole picture that makes up the performance of your organization. The key is to identify the elements that are most likely to require attention, and then to identify actions related to those elements that solve the problems and leverage the opportunities that have the highest positive impact on the business. The following table describes the elements of the MOF 4.0 SMFs and how to apply them. (This information applies to the original MOF 4.0 documentation, not the information in this pocket guide.)

Table 2-2. SMF Elements

SMF Element	How to Apply
Why use this SMF and overview?	Describes the SMF and identifies scenarios for use. Use this section to ensure that the organization has a common understanding of the meaning and context of the SMF within its lifecycle phase.
Role Types	Use this to identify the appropriate accountabilities and assign ownership to ensure that the right work gets done. Each accountability maps to one or more of the MOF service management functions that describe the processes and activities that make up the work of IT pros throughout the IT service lifecycle.
Goals	The goals identify specific outcomes and measures an organization should achieve if they are applying the SMF in their scenario—use the goals to create a common focus and a concrete set of measurements for your organization.

SMF Element	How to Apply
Outcomes	There are outcomes identified for each set of goals. Use the outcomes as a basis for measuring success—this is a starting point for determining what metrics are most relevant and useful to managing your work.
Key Terms	Four to eight applicable key terms are identified in the beginning of each SMF. Use the key terms to start a conversation with your team, and make sure to reconcile any differences in understanding—this will ensure that everyone has a common language with which to align their work.
Processes	Each SMF has three to six key processes. Combine the processes with the role types to ensure the right activities are in place and someone is accountable for the outcomes.
Activity Tables	Each SMF process has one to six key activities. The activities are described in tables. Each activity identifies key questions, inputs, outputs and best practices. • Answer the questions to drive the right decisions in your organization • Identify the correct inputs to make the activity both efficient and understood • Produce the correct outputs to ensure predictability and completions of the right elements so they can be handed off to other dependent processes. • Follow the correct best practices to see a faster road to success, better cultural adoption, and greater effectiveness.

3. The Manage Layer

Overview of the Manage Layer

* Governance, Risk, and Compliance
* Change and Configuration
* Team

The Manage Layer integrates the decision making, risk management, and change management processes that occur throughout the IT service lifecycle. It also contains the processes related to defining accountability and associated roles.

The Manage Layer represents the foundation for all phases of the lifecycle; it promotes consistency in planning and delivering IT services and provides the basis for developing and operating a resilient IT environment. This area of MOF helps IT pros coordinate processes described in the lifecycle phase SMFs, and provides guidance about:

* Establishing decision-making processes.
* Employing risk management and controls as part of all processes.
* Promoting change and configuration processes that are

appropriately controlled.

- Dividing work so that accountabilities for results are clear and do not conflict.

Goal of the Manage Layer

The primary goal of the Manage Layer is to establish an integrated approach to IT service management activities. This approach helps to coordinate processes described throughout the three lifecycle phases: Plan, Deliver, and Operate. This coordination is enhanced through:

- Development of decision making processes.
- Use of risk management and controls as part of all processes.
- Promotion of change and configuration processes that are controlled.
- Division of work so that accountabilities are clear and do not conflict.

Specific guidance is provided to increase the likelihood that:

- The investment in IT delivers the expected business value.
- Investment and resource allocation decisions involve the appropriate people.
- There is an acceptable level of risk.
- Controlled and documented processes are used.
- Accountabilities are communicated and their ownership is apparent.
- Policies and internal controls are effective and reliable.

Meeting these goals is most likely to be achieved if IT works toward:

- Explicit IT governance structures and processes.
- The IT organization and the business organization sharing a common approach to risk management.
- Regularly scheduled management reviews of policies and internal controls.

SMFs, Management Reviews, and their Relationship in the Manage Layer

Table 3-1. SMFs in the Manage Layer

SMF	Deliverable/Purpose
Governance, Risk, and Compliance	**Deliverable:** IT objectives achieved, change and risk managed and documented **Purpose:** • Support, sustain, and grow the organization while managing risks and constraints
Change and Configuration	**Deliverable:** Known configurations and predictable adaptations **Purpose:** • Ensure that changes are planned, that unplanned changes are minimal, and that IT services are robust
Team	**Deliverable:** Clear accountabilities, roles, and work assignments **Purpose:** • Agile, flexible, and scalable teams doing required work

Table 3-2. Management Reviews in the Manage Layer

Management Review	Deliverable/Purpose
Policy and Control	**Deliverable:** Identified requests for changes that will improve the management and enforcement of policies, as well as improve the management of risk and the overall control environment **Purpose:** • An understanding of how risks to achieving goals are being addressed; an assessment of the burden of control so that it can adjust appropriately for desired benefits; an evaluation of behavior as an indicator of policy communication

Management Reviews

Policy and Control Management Review

The Policy and Control MR consists of at least biannual reviews that evaluate the effectiveness of the policies and controls in place across the IT service lifecycle. The performance of IT and its partners, the reliability and trustworthiness of services provided, and the ability of IT to respond to the business are all affected by the policy and control environment. Across all phases and SMFs in the IT service lifecycle, explicit attention is given to identifying management objectives, risks that could adversely impact these objectives, and controls put in place to mitigate these risks. This MR is management's opportunity to assess policies and controls and their impact across the lifecycle in terms of achieving management objectives. The review yields a view of how well risk is being managed and of the likelihood that management objectives will be achieved, and it exemplifies "governance in action" for the Manage Layer.

Core questions for this review include:
- Are the right policies in place? (Considering management objectives, regulations, standards, and industry practices)
- Are the policies effective? (Compliance reporting, requests for changes to policies, and exceptions granted)
- Are the right controls in place? (Based on risk assessments and mitigations, events and incidents not addressed by controls, and costs and benefits of controls)
- Are controls operating effectively across the lifecycle?

Key Terms

Table 3-3. Key Terms

Term	Definition
Accountability	A way of organizing IT work that ensures the right work gets done by assigning someone who is held accountable for whether it gets done.
Change	The addition, modification, or removal of approved, supported, or baselined hardware, networks, software, applications, environments, systems, desktop builds, or associated documentation.
Change advisory board (CAB)	A cross-functional group set up to evaluate change requests for business need, priority, cost/benefit, and potential impacts to other systems or processes.
Change category	Measurement of a change's release impact on IT and the business. The change complexity and resources required, including people, money, and time, are measured to determine the category.
Change log	A log of Requests for Change (RFCs) submitted for all changes in a service that tracks the progress of each change from submission, through review, approval, implementation, and closure. A change log can be managed manually with a document or spreadsheet, or it can be managed automatically with a tool.
Change Manager	The role that has the overall management responsibility for the change management process in the IT organization.
Compliance	Processes that ensure IT's conformance with governmental regulations, laws, and company-specific policies—in other words, a means to inform individuals regarding appropriate activity and also ensure that the organization is actually doing what it has said it will do.

Configuration item (CI)	An IT component that is under configuration management control. Each CI can be composed of other CIs. CIs may vary widely in complexity, size, and type; their scope can range from an entire system (including all hardware, software, and documentation) to a single software module or a minor hardware component.
Configuration management system (CMS)	A set of tools that is used to manage IT service management data such as changes, releases, known errors, and incidents.
Contingency	A process that prepares an organization to respond coherently to planned outcomes as well as unplanned incidents.
Dedicated team	A team that exists for ongoing work, with no specific dissolution time in mind. An example of a dedicated team might be an operations team that shares ongoing maintenance for an IT service or IT component.
Definitive software library (DSL)	A secure software library where all versions of software CIs that the CAB has approved for deployment are held in their definitive, quality-controlled form.
Evidence	Testable proof that policies and processes are working as expected.
Forward Schedule of Change (FSC)	A record of upcoming approved changes, also known as a change/release calendar, which may help you understand the impact that already approved changes might have on any new proposed changes. This can also be accomplished using the service portfolio described in the Business/IT Alignment SMF.
Governance	Governance specifies who should make decisions and how, how to communicate effectively and when that should happen, and how to track IT's progress against business objectives.

IT assets	Any company-owned information, data, intellectual property, system, or machine that is used in the course of business activities.
IT controls	A specific activity performed by people or systems designed to ensure that business objectives are being met.
Mitigation	Processes or activities that are established for the purpose of reducing the potential consequences of a risk by reducing the likelihood or impact of the risk.
Post-implementation review (PIR)	A review that occurs after release of a new or updated service. This review evaluates and measures the success of the release in the production environment.
Project team	A team that is formed for a project, with a specific formation time and dissolution time. An example of a project team might be one formed to build a new IT service.

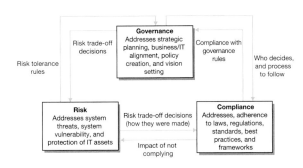

Figure 3-1. The Relationship Between Governance, Risk and Compliance

Governance, Risk, and Compliance (GRC) SMF

Policy & Control

- Governance, Risk, and Compliance
- Change and Configuration
- Team

Why use the GRC SMF?

This SMF should be useful to those who make decisions about how IT resources will be used to meet goals and deliver business value; for those needing to manage risk from many sources, not only IT security risk; and for those who need to make sure IT activities comply with regulations and directives. It addresses how to do the following:

- Establish IT governance.
- Assess, monitor, and control risk.
- Comply with directives.

What Is GRC?

IT governance is an activity that, when well performed, clarifies who holds the authority to make decisions, determines accountability for actions and responsibility for outcomes, and addresses how expected performance will be evaluated. Most organizations accomplish IT governance by creating groups, such as steering committees, that bring the right parties together to make decisions.

Organization-wide governance establishes, among other things, positive outcome and growth expectations, chosen avenues to improve customer satisfaction, new products, and market development—all areas where IT can make a significant contribution when all governance efforts are coordinated.

Governing activities happen whether planned or not. Lack of planned governance processes can result in arbitrary goal setting and decision making, political turf battles, and wasted resources from confused and conflicting efforts. Planned governance should result in:

- Consistent policies that work together effectively.
- Clear and accountable decision making with an agreed-upon plan for making tradeoffs.
- Well-communicated management objectives.
- Established expectations for performance and evaluating compliance.
- Clear expectations for acceptable behavior in pursuit of management's goals.

Risk represents possible adverse impacts on reaching goals and can arise from actions taken or not taken. Organizations use governance processes to decide priorities and the level of effort that should go into reducing the likelihood and magnitude of risk impacts.

Good governance processes seek out risk and provide open discussions and clear approaches to addressing risk. A culture of risk management helps prevent willful ignorance of risk, or intentional concealment of risk, and reduces the number of unknown risks that may result in negative consequences.

Internal controls are the processes and systems that exist to address risks and to influence—or mitigate—potential outcomes. In the most general sense, internal controls provide the means by which management objectives are reliably achieved and, in doing so, contribute to positive outcomes for stakeholders.

Compliance is a process that ensures individuals are aware of regulations, policies, and procedures that must be followed as a result of senior management's decisions. Compliance is also the evaluation of what is actually happening in the organization compared with the intended results laid out by management's objectives, policies, and regulatory requirements.

The three practices that make up GRC—governance, risk management, and compliance—share common and interrelated tasks. Because governance, risk, and compliance have overlapping areas of responsibility and process, they are more effective when they are integrated and dealt with as combined practices. This decreases data islands and silos of activity that ultimately slow down organizational responsiveness and contribute to greater risk by obscuring risk identification and producing inadequate risk impact assessments. Combining can streamline processes and provide transparency and accountability in an organization. It accomplishes this by:

- Bringing the right groups of people together (*governance*) to clarify what needs to happen and evaluate what could get in the way (*risk management*).
- Helping the organization determine resource commitments (*governance*) needed to ensure its goals are achieved (*risk management*).
- Making it clear (*governance and compliance*) what processes and activities should or should not happen (*risk management and compliance*).

- Capturing and documenting processes and their results as evidence (*compliance*).

When an organization addresses IT GRC activities, several pivotal questions help establish context. Answering these questions most likely will require conversations with groups external to IT, such as internal audit, legal, compliance, and HR.

- What is our organization's governance plan—who decides how and what to decide?
- What is our organization's risk tolerance—where can we accept more risk, and in which areas should we be more cautious?
- Are there specific regulatory and compliance issues that apply to our industry?
- What is our compliance culture—that is, how do we determine that we're doing what we said we would do?

Goals of GRC

Outcomes	Measures
Sound governance	• IT activities yield expected returns on investment • Use of IT assets meets forecasts • Decision making is timely and does not require re-examination • Confidentiality, integrity, and availability of IT assets are congruent with business needs and directives • Policies are created and managed in a timely fashion
Effective risk management	• Proactive identification and management of potential threats and vulnerabilities to the assets of the enterprise • Clear and documented process for identifying risk; determining impact and probability; prioritizing and managing through mitigation, transfer, or acceptance; and identifying appropriate controls and solutions • Confidentiality, integrity, and availability of IT assets

Compliance with regulations, laws, and policies	• Management of the impact of laws and regulations on business value realization • Identification of applicable organizational policies, laws, and regulations • Design, development, and deployment of IT assets that support compliance to laws and regulations • Reporting of measurable controls for audit and management

Table 3-4. Outcomes and Measures of the GRC SMF Goals

GRC Processes and Activities

Process 1: Establish IT Governance

Governance describes the leadership, decision-making structure, processes, and accountability that determine how an organization gets work done. Governance starts at the top, but it requires participation at every level of the organization.

IT governance can be enhanced through the clarification of objectives, roles, and responsibilities and through the application of risk management across the IT service lifecycle. This ensures that IT is able to understand business strategy and requirements, deliver value to the business while mitigating IT risks, and establish accountability throughout the lifecycle.

The CIO and other executives must make their determination that their organization's strategy and any regulation affecting corporate communication is rational and that they have set appropriate direction and policy for the rest of the organization to follow.

At the activity level, IT governance processes help align IT with the business through the decision-making process used to define actions for achieving strategic goals. This alignment happens through trade-off discussions and decision making.

An organization's governance structure and process should be established before decisions need to be made; doing this will help identify the appropriate business and IT representatives who will jointly make decisions and be held accountable. The results of governance activities ultimately affect how initiatives and technologies are chosen and provide the context for the most prized IT resource—people—to realize opportunities and benefits.

The process of establishing IT governance includes the following activities:

- Setting vision.
- Aligning IT to the business.
- Identifying regulations and standards.
- Creating policy.

Process 2: Assess, Monitor, and Control Risk

Risk management is IT's attempt to address risk while achieving management objectives. IT organizations achieve long-term success by managing risk through the effective use of internal controls.

Internal controls are specific activities performed by people or systems designed to ensure that business objectives are met. Careful design, documentation, and operation of controls are crucial at every level of the organization. Being "in control" means the chances of experiencing adverse impacts from undesirable events are at acceptable levels and that the likelihood of achieving objectives is satisfactory. Internal control is intertwined with and directly affected by an organization's governance activities.

The process of identifying risks and controls touches all aspects of the enterprise. It provides a foundation for the enterprise's compliance efforts by clearly laying out the relationship among goals, factors that might prevent achieving the goals, and how those potential events are being addressed.

Categories of risk arise throughout the various phases of the service lifecycle. They involve financial, operational, reputational, market share, revenue, and regulatory risks, as well as other risks that are more specific to a particular organization's industry (for example, healthcare) or a presently occurring activity (such as a merger or acquisition).

By approaching risk management in a way that encourages thinking about the potential consequences of activities, evaluating their impact, and then taking an explicit approach to addressing these risks, IT gains a considerable advantage. An organization cannot intelligently address risk without both IT and the business sitting down together and defining risk tolerances and control objectives. Since the consequences of risk are evaluated in terms of reaching business goals, this helps integrate IT into business discussions and tradeoffs and eliminates after the fact finger-pointing by virtue of the transparency involved in risk management.

This process includes the following activities:
- Improving processes to meet management objectives.
- Identifying risk.
- Analyzing and prioritizing risks.
- Identifying controls.
- Analyzing controls.
- Planning and scheduling implementation.
- Tracking and reporting risks and controls.
- Operating controls.
- Learning from prior efforts and updating knowledge base.

Process 3: Comply with Directives
Compliance is the application of risk management that ensures IT's conformance with company policies, governmental regulations, and industry-specific laws. Increasingly, compliance activities require

greater diligence and responsibility from IT pros. For example, many large corporations have significantly automated their financial management systems, which have resulted in the automation of internal business controls. These *application controls* are part of the compliance environment; when they are automated, they become part of the IT environment. IT pros must also be aware of *general computing controls* (for example, the separation of development and test environments), which are defined as those processes, activities, and configurations that are applied across multiple infrastructure components in order to ensure that technology performs as expected.

The compliance process is iterative; IT must continually monitor the environment, adapt to regulatory changes, and respond to management directives. IT pros should be careful to look to company policy for directives, rather than interpreting regulations without input from other areas of the business. The regulations themselves should be evaluated by various groups within the company (for example, legal, HR, and finance), who will then determine the company's stance regarding any particular regulation.

The IT pro should actively bring IT-relevant regulations to the attention of the business. These regulations can then be evaluated, the company can determine its position relative to each, and appropriate policies and directives can be constructed to guide decisions and activities. With that pathway established, the auditor will be able to take management objectives—now in the form of directives—and audit compliance to those directives.

This process includes the following activities:
- Identifying policies, laws, regulations, and contracts.
- Selecting policies, laws, regulations, and contracts.
- Assessing current compliance state.

- Setting future compliance state.
- Creating compliance plan.
- Maintaining compliance.
- Auditing compliance.

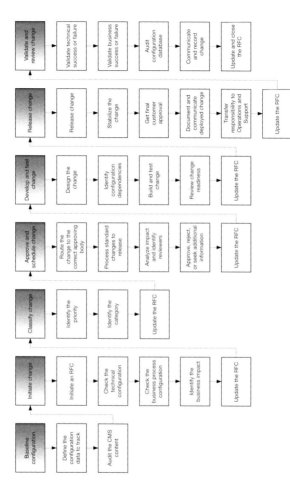

Figure 3-2. Change and Configuration SMF Process Flow

Change and Configuration SMF

* Governance, Risk, and Compliance
* Change and Configuration
* Team

Why Use the Change and Configuration SMF

This SMF should be useful for anyone who wants to understand and gain control over the changes made in IT.

It addresses how to do the following:

* Manage changes.
* Know the current state of configuration at all times.
* Reduce risk of negative impact from changes to the organization.

Goals of Change and Configuration

The primary goal of change and configuration management is to create an environment where changes can be made with the least amount of risk and impact to the organization.

The table below shows the desired outcomes of the Change and Configuration SMF goals and lists measures that you can use to gauge how successfully you have achieved these goals.

Table 3-5. Outcomes and Measures of the Change and Configuration SMF Goals

Outcomes	Measures
Have a predictable process for managing changes to the production environment to improve reliability and customer satisfaction.	• Improved reliability scores (see the Reliability SMF, and the Operations Health Review in the Operate Phase Overview) • Improved customer satisfaction scores (see the Service Review in the Plan Phase Overview)
Eliminate unnecessary change.	• Reduction in cancelled projects • Reduction in reversed changes
Reduce unintended side effects.	• Reduction in production failures
Enable IT to revert to a previous environment state in response to service disruptions by keeping accurate knowledge of the configuration and changes made.	• Number of managed service maps compared to the number of services offered • Number of items in the Configuration Management System (CMS) with historical state records • Date range of historical data maintained within the CMS (for example, previous states for the past 6 months)
Enable troubleshooting problems through an analysis of recent changes.	• Changes to production are known • Decrease time to resolve problems

Change and Configuration Processes and Activities

Process 1: Baseline the Configuration

As you begin the process of initiating and implementing a change, your first process should be to baseline the configuration so that the starting configuration is known. This baseline may be needed for rollback, disaster recovery, and understanding the impact of the proposed change.

In order to successfully manage change, an organization must also manage the configuration of the production environment. The most effective way to do this is to baseline the configuration before and after each change.

A configuration baseline is a snapshot of the IT environment that identifies its structure and underlying dependencies. The data from this snapshot should be captured and recorded in a configuration management system (CMS). A CMS can be as simple as a spreadsheet or as complex as an integrated set of tools that includes a database.

A CMS provides:
- A way to understand, control, and predict the consequences of change.
- An accurate and comprehensive representation of the state of the production environment.
- A history of previous states to support efforts to analyze and remedy problems.

IT professionals can use the CMS throughout the change process by:
- Reviewing it as part of evaluating a new request for change (RFC) in order to understand the impact of the proposed change.
- Updating it with approved RFCs so that this knowledge can be used in evaluating other RFCs.
- Updating it with released changes so that this knowledge can be used in troubleshooting any problems that arise after the change.
- Using it to confirm a known good state for rolling back any changes that have unexpected negative impacts.

A CMS contains information about configuration items (CIs), which are IT components that are important in understanding the state of the production environment. Each CI may be composed of other CIs and can vary widely in complexity, size, and type—from an entire system (including all hardware, software, and documentation) to a single software module or a minor hardware component. All versions of software CIs that the change advisory board (CAB) has approved for deployment should be contained in their definitive, quality-controlled form in a definitive software library (DSL). This is a secure software library that provides a known good source of the software used in production.

Baselining configuration can be a major undertaking. One option is to baseline as you make changes so that eventually the entire production configuration is known.

This process includes the following activities:
- Defining and collecting the configuration data to track in the CMS each time a new type of CI is added to the configuration.
- Auditing the CMS content.

Process 2: Initiate the Change
After baselining the configuration, you can initiate the change.

Change requests can come from many sources, including:
- End-user requests. (see the Customer Service SMF and Service Alignment Management Review in the Plan Phase Overview)
- Business initiatives. (see the Business/IT Alignment SMF)
- IT initiatives. (see the Business/IT Alignment SMF and Operational Health Management Review in the Operate Phase Overview)
- Problem analysis. (see the Problem Management SMF)
- Service monitoring. (see the Service Monitoring and Control SMF)

All change requests need to be evaluated for impact and benefit to the organization.

The activities involved in initiating the change include:
- Initiating an RFC.
- Checking the technical configuration.
- Checking the business process configuration.
- Identifying the business impact.
- Updating the RFC.

Process 3: Classify the Change

The next process is to classify the requested change.

After the RFC is initiated, the next process is to classify the request.

The activities involved in classifying the change include:
- Identifying the priority of the change.
- Identifying the category of the change.
- Checking and validating the configuration.
- Assessing the risk and updating the risk value in the RFC.
- Updating the RFC.

Process 4: Approve and Schedule the Change

The next process is to have the change approved.

Approval of a change is driven by its category. Approval for a significant or major change usually begins by presenting the change to the appropriate approving body—a team of reviewers typically known as the change advisory board (CAB). These are key people who represent many perspectives and who will be held accountable for the results of the change. The considerations involved in establishing the CAB are discussed in the Governance, Risk, and Compliance SMF. Emergency changes are normally reviewed by an emergency committee of the CAB for fast-track approval.

It is up to the CAB to determine if the change should:

- Be approved and scheduled.
- Be refused and ended.
- Be returned to earlier processes of this SMF for further clarification and consideration.

Understanding the potential impact of change is fundamental when making approval decisions. The inputs for the approval process include:

- Previously determined risk tolerance. (This is explained in the Governance, Risk, and Compliance SMF and the Policy SMF.)
- The category of the change—Standard, Minor, Significant, Major, or Emergency—which summarizes the complexity and resources required, including people, money, and time.
- The potential impact of the change on the organization's configuration and users, including service downtime.

This information helps in the identification and selection of appropriate reviewers with sufficient knowledge and authority to make a decision.

Standard changes require little effort to implement, carry a low level of risk, and have predefined approval. If a change has been classified as a standard change, it promptly moves through the minimally required approval and documentation process to release. Minor changes can be approved by the Change Manager. All other change categories require approval of the CAB.

The methods for reaching a decision to approve or reject a change should be determined before the CAB reviews the change. Depending on the governance models chosen by an organization, voting is often employed to reach a decision and move the change into another activity or to stop it altogether.

Once the CAB reaches a decision, it is important that the conclusion be documented in the RFC so that the knowledge gained during the processing of the change is captured. This allows for more efficient auditing of the change management process as well as providing information that can be used in additional iterations through the change process.

This process includes the following activities:
- Routing the change to the correct approving body.
- Processing standard changes to release.
- Analyzing the impact of the change and identifying reviewers.
- Approving or rejecting the change, or seeking additional information.
- Updating the RFC.

Process 5: Develop and Test the Change
Once a change has been approved, development and then testing of the proposed change can start. These are activities that coincide with the Deliver Phase of the IT service lifecycle. They focus on ensuring that IT services are envisioned, planned, built, stabilized, and released in line with business requirements and the customer's specifications.

Developing and testing a change are activities that tie directly to the Deliver Phase of the IT service lifecycle. More information about developing and testing a change can be found in the Deliver Phase Overview.

Low-risk and minimal-effort changes can go through this process and the next process very quickly. More complex changes should follow the processes outlined in the Deliver SMFs. Both sets of processes follow a similar path. Follow these guidelines for each change request category:

- **Standard Change:** Follow the established procedures for the standard change.
- **Minor Change:** Follow the processes for minor changes outlined in this document. See the Deliver SMFs for more detail if needed.
- **Significant** or **Major Change:** See the Deliver SMFs.
- **Emergency Change:** Use where necessary to quickly get an essential service back up and running, Testing may be delayed until after the release of the change. Be sure to complete the testing to confirm that there are no unknown issues caused by the change. Use caution when dealing with emergency changes, as risk levels are generally higher.

This process includes the following activities:
- Designing the change.
- Identifying configuration dependencies.
- Building and testing the change.
- Reviewing the readiness of the change for release.
- Updating the RFC.

Process 6: Release the Change
Once the changed has been built, tested, and reviewed for release readiness, it is time to release the change.

The Release Readiness Management Review marks the end of the testing of a change. At this point, the process of releasing the change begins. Releasing the change coincides with the Deploy SMF in the Deliver Phase of the IT service lifecycle.

This process includes the following activities:
- Releasing the change and any accompanying site components into the production environment.
- Stabilizing the release.
- Getting final customer approval of the change.

- Documenting the released change and communicating the impact to users.
- Transferring responsibility from the project team that built the change to Operations and Support.
- Updating the configuration database.
- Updating the RFC.

Process 7: Validate and Review the Change

The final process is to validate that the change has been released correctly and to review the effectiveness of the change.

After the team has successfully released the change into the production environment, the next important process is to validate the release and then review it. The goal of validation is to verify that the change has actually been released as expected. The goal of reviewing the change—typically called a post-implementation review (PIR)—is to determine whether the change has had the desired effect and has met the requirements from the original RFC.

Determining whether the released change has been effective and has achieved the desired results requires monitoring the change in the production environment. For a small change, this might be a matter of checking on the desired functionality. Larger changes might require monitoring of network and server information, performance data, event logs, and response times.

After the release of the change has been validated, the PIR can be performed. The results of the PIR should include:

- A success/failure decision on the change implementation.
- A review of how the change was released and whether it was implemented on time and on budget.
- Documentation of the lessons learned from the change process.

This process includes the following activities:

- Validating the technical success or failure of the change.
- Validating the business success or failure of the change.
- Auditing the configuration database.
- Communicating and recording the change.
- Updating and closing the RFC.

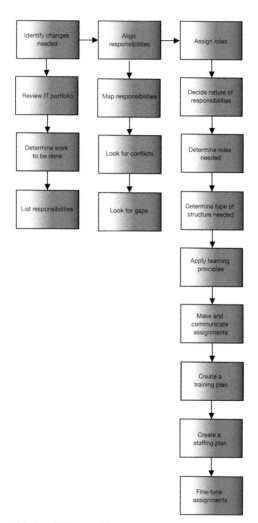

Figure 3-3. Team SMF Process Flow

Team SMF

- Governance, Risk, and Compliance
- Change and Configuration
- Team ◄

Why Use the Team SMF?

This SMF will be useful for anyone who is responsible for ensuring that someone is ultimately accountable for the work required to effectively deliver IT services.

It addresses how to:

- Understand the key principles for effectively organizing IT.
- Understand accountabilities and role types.
- Identify organizational changes needed.
- Align responsibilities.
- Assign roles.

Goals of the Team SMF

The MOF Team SMF demonstrates how to build and maintain an IT organization that is:

- Accountable: ensures that required IT work gets done

- Responsible: identifies who will do required IT work through:
  - Creating role types and roles
  - Establishing principles and best practices
  - Identifying who is best for each role
- Flexible: built around agile physical and virtual teams
- Scalable: able to meet the needs of different-sized organizations

Table 3-6. Outcomes and Measures of the Team SMF Goals

Outcomes	Measures
Accountability assigned for all required IT work	• Upper management knows and understands accountabilities • All accountabilities are assigned to someone
Responsibility assigned for all required IT work	• All work is owned and responsibilities are clear • Staff members know what they need to do
Accountability and responsibility assignments are clearly communicated	• IT professionals know their roles and who they need to coordinate with
Assignments are flexible enough to meet changing business needs	• Organization can change quickly to adapt to business needs • Services drive the assignments (rather than assignments driving the services provided)

Key Terms

Table 3-7. Key Terms

Term	Definition
Accountability	A way of organizing IT work that ensures the right work gets done by assigning someone who is held accountable for whether it gets done.
Responsibility	The details of the work that has to be done by a role type.
Role	A set of responsibilities in an IT organization. Depending on the effort required and the size of the organization, a single person might perform a single role or multiple roles, or a single role might be performed by multiple persons.
Role type	A generic variation of the term role, used to indicate that a particular role might be similar and serve roughly the same purposes in different IT organizations, but called by different names.
Team	A group of people linked in a common purpose, generally for conducting complex tasks that have interdependent subtasks.

Accountabilities and Role Types

At the heart of the Team SMF is a set of accountabilities for ensuring that the right work gets done.

Each accountability maps to one or more of the MOF service management functions that describe the processes and activities that make up the work of IT pros throughout the IT service lifecycle.

Table 3-8. Accountabilities and Role Types

Accountability	Phase or Layer	SMF	Nature of Work
Support	Operate Phase	Customer Service; Problem Management	Interrupt-driven
Operations	Operate Phase	Operations Management; Service Monitoring and Control	Plan-driven, repetitive
Solutions	Deliver Phase	Envision; Project Planning; Build; Stabilize; Deploy	Plan-driven, short-term
Architecture	Plan Phase	Reliability	Plan-driven, long-term
Service	Plan Phase	Business/IT Alignment	Plan-driven, long-term
Compliance	Manage Layer	Governance, Risk, and Compliance	Plan-driven, repetitive
Management	Manage Layer	Financial Management; Business/IT Alignment Policy; Governance, Risk, and Compliance; Change and Configuration Team	Plan-driven, long-term

Support Accountability

The Support Accountability addresses role types that are important to two SMFs from the Operate Phase of the IT service lifecycle: Customer Service and Problem Management. The nature of the Support role-cluster is ad-hoc and reactive, responding to service outages and customer requests when they appear. This asks for IT staff that is competent in communicating with the end-users and in analyzing quickly what actions need to be taken. Within the role-cluster there should also be sufficient resources to perform a deeper investigation of problems in order to prevent new outages from happening.

Associated Role Types:

- Customer Services Representative
- Incident Resolver
- Problem Analyst
- Problem Manager
- Customer Service Manager

Operations Accountability

The Operations Accountability addresses role types that are important to two SMFs that are also in the Operate Phase of the IT service lifecycle: Operations and Service Monitoring and Control. The nature of the Operations cluster is more repetitive and proactive, executing maintenance tasks that will prevent possible issues in the future as well as ensuring performance in the short term. The focus of the Operations cluster is therefore more on the systems and applications in the infrastructure than on customers and users. The activities of the Operations cluster are often a candidate for automation.

Associated Role Types:

- Operator
- Administrator
- Technology Area Manager
- Monitoring Manager
- Scheduling Manager
- Operations Manager

Solutions Accountability

The Solutions Accountability addresses the role types that are important to five SMFs in the Deliver Phase of the IT service lifecycle: Envision, Project Planning, Build, Stabilize, and Deploy. The Solutions role-cluster performs activities that are part of projects deployed by the organization. These activities are, in principle, able to be planned using project management methods, but not repetitive. This makes standardization and automation difficult. Where the workload of most role-clusters are predictable and stable, this is not the case for the Solutions role-cluster. It depends on the number and scale of the projects in the portfolio.

Associated Role Types:

- Developer
- Tester
- Product Manager
- User Experience
- Operations Experience
- Release Management
- Test Manager
- Program Manager
- Solution Manager

Architecture Accountability

The Architecture Accountability addresses the role types that are important to the Reliability SMF, which is located in the Plan Phase of the IT service lifecycle. The activities of the Architecture role-cluster are plan-able and will most often relate to the business cycle of the company. The Architecture Accountability will be about long term planning of performance, capacity and reliability of the IT services as well as the overall design of these services. This requires the ability to look beyond the day-to-day operation and to envision possible new solutions to meet changing customer demands.

Associated Role Types:
- Architect
- Reliability Manager
- Architecture Manager

Service Accountability

The Service Accountability addresses the role types that are important to the Business/IT Alignment SMF, which is located in the Plan Phase of the IT service lifecycle. Business/IT Alignment focuses on strengthening the alignment between IT departments and the larger organizations within which they exist. The main focus of the Service role-cluster will be on the dialogue between the IT organization, the customers and the suppliers. The role-cluster will work with the customer to clarify their perception on the current IT service and how to improve this as well as their future demands for new IT services. In order to keep control on the growing complexity of IT service delivery it is apparent that the Service role-cluster deals with supplier and contract management.

Associated Role Types:

- Account Manager
- Supplier Manager
- Portfolio Manager
- Service Level Manager

Compliance Accountability

The Compliance Accountability addresses the role types that are important to the Governance, Risk, and Compliance (GRC) SMF, which is located in the Manage Layer of the IT service lifecycle. GRC focuses on providing IT services that are effective, efficient, and compliant by regular audits and checks on how the IT service is delivered. In order to ensure that the IT organization is compliant to internal and external rules, regulations, agreements, and laws the Compliance role-cluster will be responsible for regular assessments to signal possible breaches and to prevent compliance issues from happening.

Associated Role Types:

- Assurance & Reporting
- Internal Control Manager
- Legal
- Risk & Compliance Manager

Management Accountability

The Management Accountability addresses the role types that are important to five SMFs, three of them from the Plan Phase of the IT service lifecycle, and two of them from the Manage Layer. Those SMFs are Financial Management; Business/IT Alignment; Policy; Governance, Risk, and Compliance (GRC); and Change and Configuration. The Management role-cluster will set the policies and regulations for all to follow (with regular checks by the Compliance role-cluster). They also create the overall strategy of the

IT organization which is then used by the other teams as guidance for their day-to-day work. The Management role-cluster will be responsible for maintaining the agenda of the IT organization as well as the knowledge and information needed to perform.

Associated Role Types:
- IT Executive Officer
- IT Manager
- IT Policy Manager
- Change Manager
- Configuration Administrator

Team SMF Process and Activities
The Team SMF does not have a true process flow in the same sense that, for example, the Customer Service SMF does. However, there are three basic processes to ensuring that an IT organization has its people and work aligned, and these can serve as a stage-by-stage approach to building a set of accountabilities, role types, and responsibilities for an update or fine tuning.

Process 1: Identify changes needed
Many factors can drive a change in the roles and responsibilities in IT. Changes may occur in the staffing, skills, and training required for certain tasks or in the frequency or methods of accomplishing tasks. New markets, technology, or policies can all influence responsibilities.

The primary activities in identifying whether such changes are needed are:
- Review IT portfolio.
- Determine work to be done.
- List responsibilities.

Process 2: Align responsibilities

Review the upcoming IT demand changes to determine what responsibilities need to be added, deleted, or adjusted. This may be a change in volume that would drive reassignments, or it may be a change in what kind of work is done.

The primary activities involved in aligning responsibilities are:
- Map responsibilities.
- Look for conflicts.
- Look for gaps.

Process 3: Assign roles

When new responsibilities have been identified, they need to be assigned to roles and teams formed. There are many ways to form teams. Depending on organizational culture, patterns of work, and the skills and personalities available in the group, some types of teams work better than others. Be clear about responsibility ownership.

The primary activities required for assigning roles are:
- Decide the nature of the responsibilities.
- Determine the roles needed.
- Determine the type of structure needed.
- Make and communicate assignments.
- Create a training plan.
- Create a staffing plan.
- Fine tune assignments.

Improving Management in Your Organization

Use the following checklist to determine the right set of priorities for your organization. To support the right set of decisions, refer to the MOF guidance, which provides key questions, inputs, outputs and best practices that support decision making: www.microsoft.com/mof.

Governance, Risk, and Compliance SMF Checklist

- Establish IT governance.
- Assess, monitor, and control risk.
- Comply with directives.

Key Questions

- Have you factored in risk tolerance in the decision-making process?
- Do you think you are taking a very explicit approach in addressing the risks that you have identified?
- Do you refer to company policies for directives and not just interpret regulations without any inputs from other business areas?

Change and Configuration SMF Checklist

- Baseline the configuration.
- Initiate the change.
- Classify the change.
- Approve and schedule the change.
- Develop and test the change.
- Release the change.
- Validate and review the change.

Key Questions

- Are you recording the data from configuration baseline in a configuration management system?
- Are the change requests being evaluated for their impact and benefit to the organization?
- Do you have a method in place for reaching a decision on the change request?
- Did you exercise a higher degree of caution when dealing with emergency changes?
- Have you properly documented the released change and communicated the impact to users?
- Were you able to monitor the change in the production environment?

Team SMF Checklist

- Identify changes needed.
- Align responsibilities.
- Assign roles.

Key Questions

- What do you think are the upcoming changes that will have an effect on IT in your organization?
- What responsibilities are going to be changed upon your review of the IT demand changes?
- Have you been clear about responsibility ownership when forming teams?

4. The Plan Phase

- Business/IT Alignment
- Reliability
- Policy
- Financial Management

Service Alignment

Portfolio

Overview of the Plan Phase

What does business want from IT? Services that are reliable, compliant, cost-effective, and that continually adapt to the ever-changing needs of the business. The Plan Phase is where business and IT work as partners to determine how IT will be focused to deliver services that enable the organization to succeed. Doing that requires:

- Understanding the business strategy and requirements and how the current IT services support the business.
- Understanding what reliability means to this organization and how it will be measured and improved by reviewing and taking action where needed.
- Understanding what policy requirements exist and how they impact the IT strategy.
- Providing the financial structure to support the IT work and drive the right decisions.
- Creating an IT strategy to provide value to the business strategy and making the portfolio decisions that support that IT strategy.

The IT strategy is the plan that aligns the organization's objectives, policies, and procedures into a cohesive approach to deliver the desired set of services that support the business strategy. Quality, costs, and reliability need to be balanced in order to achieve the organization's desired outcomes. During the Plan Phase, IT pros work with the business to align business objectives and functions with IT's capabilities and constraints. The IT strategy is the result of this alignment and serves as a roadmap for IT. The strategy continually evolves and improves as organizations improve their optimizing skills and ability to adapt to business changes.

The figure above illustrates the position of the Plan Phase within the IT service lifecycle.

Goals of the Plan Phase

The primary goals of the Plan Phase are to provide guidance to IT groups on how to continually plan for, and optimize, the IT service strategy and to ensure that the delivered services are:

- Valuable and compelling.
- Predictable and reliable.
- Compliant.
- Cost-effective.
- Adaptable to the changing needs of the business.

SMFs, Management Reviews, and their Relationship in the Plan Phase

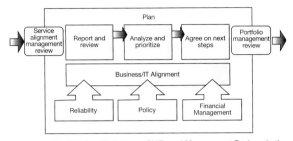

Figure 4-1. The Relationship between SMFs and Management Reviews in the Plan Phase

Table 4-1. SMFs in the Plan Phase

SMF	Deliverable/Purpose
Business/IT Alignment	**Deliverable:** IT service strategy **Purpose:** • Deliver the right set of compelling services as perceived by the business
Reliability	**Deliverable:** IT standards **Purpose:** • Ensure that service capacity, service availability, service continuity, and data integrity are aligned to the business needs in a cost-effective manner
Policy	**Deliverable:** IT policies **Purpose:** • Define and manage IT policies required for the implementation of business policies and effectiveness of IT
Financial Management	**Deliverable:** IT financial plan and measurement **Purpose:** • Accurately predict, account for, and optimize costs of required resources to deliver an end-to-end service to ensure correct investments

Table 4-2. Management Reviews in the Plan Phase

Management Reviews	Deliverable/Purpose
Service Alignment	**Deliverable:** Proposal of new services, changes to existing services (such as service improvements) that are larger than standard changes, and decommissioning of features and services **Purpose:** • Assess the customers' experience of IT services compared to service goals as well as how IT is delivering that experience in terms of reliability, compliance, cost effectiveness, and value realization
Portfolio	**Deliverable:** Initial project charter **Purpose:** • Understand the concepts and requirements of proposed IT service changes; decide whether to invest further in the development of those concepts, and approve a preliminary project vision and scope that will move a project forward into the Envision SMF in the Deliver Phase of the lifecycle

Management Reviews

Service Alignment Review

The Service Alignment MR provides an important view into the Plan Phase of the IT service lifecycle. It is focused on understanding the state of supply and demand for IT services and directing investments to make sure that the business value of IT is realized. The review should asses the customers' experience of IT services compared to service goals as well as how IT is delivering that experience in terms of reliability, compliance, cost effectiveness, and value realization.

To deliver an effective review of Service Alignment, IT management must orchestrate several activities and then participate in the review itself. Participation is needed from operations, service managers, the business, key stakeholders in IT initiatives, as well as parties responsible for developing business cases and ensuring value realization from IT investments. The review serves a key governance function in terms of bringing together people who have decision-making authority and those with the information needed for analysis. The result should be decisions to proceed with certain initiatives and changes, rejection of requests, or the determination that additional information is needed for decision making.

It is important that these reviews are seen as a form of internal control. To this end, documentation of the review should include who the participants are, the goal of the review, the decisions made, the proposed initiatives and changes that resulted, and the intended outcomes of initiatives and changes (how they will support management objectives).

Additionally, the review presents the opportunity to identify barriers that decrease business/IT alignment or inhibit innovation to the degree that business value is negatively affected.

Portfolio Management Review

The Portfolio MR acts as a gateway in the Plan Phase of the IT service lifecycle. It focuses on understanding the concepts and requirements of proposed IT service changes, on deciding whether to invest further in the development of those concepts, and approving a preliminary project vision and scope that will move a project forward into the Envision SMF in the Deliver Phase of the lifecycle. The Portfolio MR results in business and IT agreeing on expectations for value and impact of the proposed work. The review establishes the basis for how changes to the portfolio and its value to the business will be measured and evaluated.

The intentions of this MR are to determine that IT is working on the right things to positively impact the business and clarifying what capabilities of the business will be enabled or improved by the proposed projects. The review also confirms stakeholder understanding and support by establishing expectations for scope, value realization, and the intent of initiatives in terms of impact on the organization, customers, and the IT portfolio.

The alignment of business and IT is improved by:
- Defining the context of the project.
- Identifying and clarifying areas of ambiguity before proceeding.
- Judging the fit with the current portfolio.
- Taking into account existing services and initiatives in the pipeline that will result in the "to-be" IT environment.

Participation in this MR should involve an advisory board of those with the authority and knowledge required to make the relevant investment decisions. This board should include the executive sponsor for the project, business stakeholders, project team members, and representatives of enterprise architecture, finance, and the project management office, if one exists.

Key Terms

Table 4-3. Key Terms

Term	Definition
Availability management	The process of managing a service or application so that it is accessible when users need it. Availability is typically measured in percentage of uptime; downtime refers to periods of system unavailability.
Business continuity planning	The process for planning and practicing IT's response to a disaster or disruptive event. These activities span the organization; beyond just IT, continuity planning affects Finance, Operations, and Human Resources (HR) functions.
Business relationship management	The ongoing process that ensures that the organization and IT remain in sync with respect to common goals and strategies.
Demand management	The process of aligning an organization's supply of IT resources to meet service demands forecasted by the business.
Capacity management	In the context of IT, capacity refers to the processing or performance capability of a service or system. Capacity management is the process used to ensure that current and future business IT needs are met in a cost-effective manner. This process is made up of three sub-processes: business, service, and resource capacity management.
IT alignment	A state when the technical and business goals and strategies of the IT organization completely match the goals and strategies of the overall business.
IT service continuity management	The process of assessing and managing IT risks that can significantly affect the delivery of services to the business.

Term	Definition
IT service strategy	The plan that aligns an organization's objectives, policies, and procedures into a cohesive approach to deliver services that support business strategy.
Operating level agreement (OLA)	An internal agreement between one or more IT teams that supports the requirements set forth in the service level agreements (SLAs).
Operational costs	Costs resulting from the day-to-day running of IT—for example, staff costs, hardware maintenance, and electricity. Also referred to as non-discretionary spending.
Policy	A deliberate plan of action to guide decisions and achieve rational outcomes. (This definition deals with human-readable descriptions of desired behavior, not machine-readable descriptions).
Procedure	A detailed description of how work will be done by people or systems. It is the method for applying and implementing policy.
Process	A set of interrelated tasks that, taken together, produce a defined, desired result. Policies are translated into systems, resources, and processes to operate the business.
Return on investment (ROI)	The ratio of money gained or lost on an investment relative to the amount of money invested.
Service catalog	A comprehensive list of services, including priorities of the business and corresponding SLAs.
Service level agreement (SLA)	A written agreement documenting required levels of service. The SLA is agreed upon by the IT service provider and the business, or by the IT service provider and a third-party provider. SLAs should list the metrics and measures that define success for both IT and the organization.

Term	Definition
Service level management	The process of defining and managing performance through monitoring, reporting, and reviewing the required, agreed-upon level of service.
Service portfolio	An internal repository that defines IT services and categorizes them as currently in service, in queue to be developed, or in queue to be decommissioned. All services support a specific business process or function.
Total cost of ownership (TCO)	The total cost of an item over its useful lifetime. TCO takes into account not only the purchase price, but also implementation and training costs, management costs, and support costs.
Underpinning contract (UC)	A legally binding contract in place of, or in addition to, an SLA. This type of contract is with a third-party service provider responsible for building service deliverables for the SLA.
Value realization	The identification, definition, monitoring, and evaluation of targeted business benefits that result from planned IT activities.

Business/IT Alignment SMF

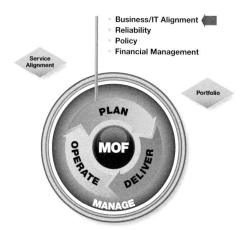

Why Use the Business/IT Alignment SMF?

This SMF should be useful for anyone wanting to better align business and IT strategy to ensure that IT services provide business value. It provides an understanding of the fundamental process steps involved and describes the context of aligning business and IT goals, developing an IT service strategy, identifying an IT portfolio of work, and establishing methods of keeping business and IT aligned.

It addresses how to do the following:

- Define IT service strategy.
- Identify and map IT services.
- Measure demand and manage business requests.
- Develop an IT service portfolio.
- Establish service level management.

Goals of Business/IT Alignment

The goals of the Business/IT Alignment SMF are to ensure that:

- IT strategy is aligned to an organization's broader goals and objectives.
- Delivered IT services are effective and efficient in meeting the organization's needs.
- IT offerings and services are aligned to the business goals.

The achievement of these goals should result in several specific, measurable outcomes, which are detailed in the table below.

Table 4-4. Outcomes and Measures of the Business/IT Alignment SMF Goals

Outcomes	Measures
The business considers IT as a strategic asset.	• The business continues to invest in enhancements or new services. • The business consults with IT as part of strategic decisions, acquisitions, or new directions.
IT has a strategic plan.	• The business and IT publish and measure an annual IT service strategy. The strategy articulates the linkages between IT goals and the business goals and outlines measurements, budget, risks, and a plan for execution.
IT has an understanding of its capabilities and resources.	• IT has a predictable model for estimating resource consumption and the adoption of new technologies. • IT measures business demand of services offered and uses this information for planning purposes.
IT has a set of defined services and projects that support the strategic plan.	• IT has a published service portfolio that identifies all projects. • IT has a published service catalog that identifies and describes all services offered to the organization.

Business/IT Alignment Processes and Activities

One of the most important things that IT can provide to any organization is a positive overall impact—to business outcomes, to objectives, to the bottom line. But this can happen only if IT's service strategy is aligned to the goals and objectives of the organization. To assist in this process, the Business/IT Alignment SMF focuses on the following processes:

- Define an IT service strategy.
- Identify and map services.
- Identify IT service demand and manage business requests.
- Develop and evaluate the IT service portfolio.
- Manage service levels.

Business Alignment acts as the coordinating SMF in the Plan Phase, responsible for taking input from the other SMFs within the phase—Reliability, Financial Management, and Policy—to drive business value and the IT service strategy. Reliability, Financial Management, and Policy are ongoing functions that support the planning and optimization of the IT service strategy.

Process 1: Define an IT Service Strategy

An IT service strategy determines which services are required to support business goals and objectives. Business and IT management must carefully discern which initiatives offer the highest business value while ensuring the availability of necessary resources and the commitment to deliver on the investment.

A successful service strategy will ensure that:

- IT goals are aligned to business goals.
- Annual IT initiatives that support business goals have been identified.
- There is agreement on both the strategy and a corresponding plan for achieving the goals and initiatives.

- The strategy is assessed against business outcomes.
- Opportunities for improvement are identified.

Process 2: Identify and Map Services

Service maps are used throughout the IT organization to clarify the dependencies between SLAs, OLAs, technologies, customers, and the impact to the service delivery. They identify the resources necessary to deliver a service described in the service catalog, who delivers that service, and who consumes it.

A service map represents a service from the perspective of the business and the user. It is divided into five sections:

- **Customers**. A categorized list of individuals and groups who use the service.
- **Hardware**. The hardware platforms necessary for service delivery.
- **Applications**. The operating system(s) and other applications the service requires.
- **Settings**. The configuration settings necessary for the service to function.
- **Internal/external services**. The components that help ensure availability for the service.

Process 3: Identify Demand and Manage Business Requests

Demand and request management analysis is a process that articulates how IT services are being used and requested by the organization and how future trends might affect the services. Demand management data helps managers plan and account for their IT expenditures, understand the IT business services they are receiving in return, and participate in decisions about future projects and resource allocation.

A fully matured demand and request management process will ensure that:

- There is a predictable process for managing requests.
- There is a consistent model for measuring current demand.
- There is a method of analyzing requests and current service capacity.

Process 4: Develop and Evaluate IT Service Portfolio

When an organization has finalized its IT service strategy, the business and IT must determine which projects and services best support that strategy. The IT service portfolio is the list of those projects and services. Ensuring that the right services and projects are included in the portfolio requires the following components:

- Proposed projects aligned to IT strategy initiatives
- A list of projects in the queue, implemented services, and services slated for decommission
- A prioritization and approval process for new projects
- A measurement system for determining the value of services in relation to business goals

The IT service portfolio drives the alignment of IT resource consumption, the operating budget, and investment strategies that support the IT service strategy. The portfolio's primary users are the business and IT leaders responsible for realizing business value from the investment in IT.

Process 5: Service Level Management

If IT strategy is to be seamlessly aligned to the organization's strategy, IT must manage the ongoing delivery and enhancement of its services—this is the goal of Service Level Management. Service Level Management ensures that ongoing requirements, communications, and expectations between business and IT are proactively managed. Service Level Management is also responsible for ensuring that internal IT expectations are being met.

The service catalog sets the standards against which expectations, improvements, and performance metrics are measured. SLAs and operating level agreements (OLAs) ensure that agreements are in place to support the offerings within the service catalog.

IT Service Catalog:
- Communicates standard IT services to customers in clear, familiar terms.
- Provides a centralized channel through which end users can request standardized, typical IT service bundles.

Operating Level Agreements (OLAs):
- Communicate and document the agreed-upon expectations of dependent IT services.
- Are agreed upon between IT teams.

Service Level Agreements (SLAs):
- Communicate and document the agreed-upon expectations of business-facing IT services.
- Are agreed upon between business and IT representatives.

Underpinning Contract (UC):
- Ensures there is a contract between suppliers, third parties, and the organization.
- Communicates and documents the agreed-upon expectations between the suppliers, third parties, and the organization.

Planning	Implementation	Monitoring and improving plans
Define service requirements	Develop availability plan	Monitor
Plan and analyze	Develop capacity plan	Report and analyze trends
	Develop data security plan	Review reliabiity
	Develop disaster recovery plan	
	Develop monitoring plan	
	Review and approve plans	

Figure 4-2. Reliability SMF Process Flow

Reliability SMF

Business/IT Alignment
Reliability
Policy
Financial Management

Service Alignment

Portfolio

PLAN
MOF
OPERATE
DELIVER
MANAGE

Why Use the Reliability SMF?

A reliable service or system is dependable, requires minimal maintenance, will perform without interruption, and allows users to quickly access the resources they need. These characteristics are not only true for business-as-usual conditions; they must also apply during times of business change and growth and during unexpected events. Ensuring reliability involves three high-level processes:

- **Planning**. Gathering and translating business requirements into IT measures
- **Implementation**. Building the various plans and ensuring that they can meet expectations
- **Monitoring and Improvement**. Proactively monitoring and managing the plans and making necessary adjustments

The Reliability SMF should be useful for anyone who wants to understand, set targets, and measure IT service reliability.

It addresses creating plans for the following:

- Confidentiality
- Continuity
- Integrity
- Capacity
- Availability

Goals of Reliability

The Reliability SMF ensures that service capacity, service availability, service continuity, data integrity, and confidentiality are aligned to the business needs in a cost-effective manner.

Table 4-5. Outcomes and Measures of the Reliability SMF Goals

Outcomes	Measures
IT capacity aligned to business needs	• Proactive capacity plan • No capacity-related service disruptions • Procurement/purchasing plan developed and adhered to
Services available to users when needed	• Proactive, cost-justified availability plan • Reduction in service failures • Minimized service disruption from anticipated failures
Critical business services available during significant failures	• IT disaster recovery aligned to business continuity plan • Tested, trusted, recovery plan supported by the business
Data integrity and confidentiality maintained	• Data classified and managed according to business policy • No exceptions to data handling and integrity requirements

Reliability Processes and Activities

Figure 4-2 illustrates the process flow for the Reliability SMF. This flow consists of the following processes:

- Planning
- Implementation
- Monitoring and improving plans

Process 1: Planning

Thorough planning is the first process in achieving reliability.

Activities include:

- Define service requirements.
- Plan and analyze business and technical requirements.

The first activity in planning for Reliability Management is to clearly understand and document the business requirements for the service. Understanding the business objectives allows IT to prioritize and allocate resources to the service and to better align technology investment decisions with the organization's priorities. IT gathers these requirements by engaging the business through an ongoing relationship management process.

The second activity in planning focuses on the effort and investment that IT must make to ensure that business expectations are met. Doing this successfully involves understanding both the target IT environment and the specifications for the new service: how these align with each other, how the new service will affect the current environment, and where there are significant technical or resource capability gaps.

Process 2: Implementing

Implementing reliability involves the following activities:

- Developing various plans: availability, capacity, information security, disaster recovery, monitoring
- Reviewing and adjusting the plans for suitability before approving them

These reliability plans address the traditional objectives of availability, disaster recovery, capacity, data integrity, and monitoring functions. They can exist separately or be combined, depending on specific organizational requirements and scale. For larger, more complex organizations, it might be appropriate to retain some or all of the traditional plans individually. However, they should be managed collectively so as to take advantage of common objectives and technical solutions. This strategy helps the organization achieve higher reliability more cost-effectively.

IT management uses the requirements from the planning process to build corresponding plans that will allow their departments to meet or exceed delivery expectations. Activities and tasks performed during this process can include:

- Analysis of existing infrastructure and how the new service will affect it.
- Evaluation of new technologies that can help IT achieve the desired outcomes.
- Validating that the plans meet delivery expectations and align to infrastructure standards.
- Adapting plans as business needs change.

The outcome of implementing results in the following plans:

- Availability
- Integrity – Data Integrity Plan
- Confidentiality – Data Integrity Plan

- Continuity – Disaster Recovery Plan
- Capacity – Monitoring Plan

Process 3: Monitoring and Improving Plans

The third process of Reliability Management is monitoring and improving plans, an ongoing procedure that ensures that the first two processes have been followed, that metrics are reported on, that exceptions to targets are tracked, and that improvements are fed back into the Plan phase. Proper monitoring ensures that either the original objectives are being achieved or steps are being taken to improve reliability or adjust business expectations. This process includes the following activities:

- Monitor service reliability.
- Report and analyze trends in service reliability.
- Review reliability.

Business requirements and technology are both subject to frequent change. This iterative review and reporting function helps to promote an ongoing alignment between actual service delivery and business requirements, ensuring that these reliability functions are up to date and relevant.

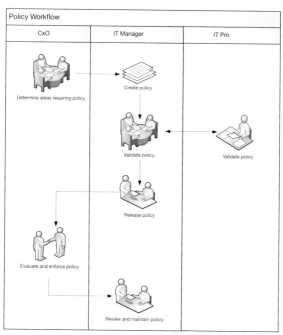

Policy Workflow		
CxO	IT Manager	IT Pro

Determine areas requiring policy

Create policy

Validate policy

Validate policy

Release policy

Evaluate and enforce policy

Review and maintain policy

Figure 4-3. Policy SMF Process Flow

Policy SMF

- Business/IT Alignment
- Reliability
- Policy
- Financial Management

Service Alignment

Portfolio

PLAN
MOF
OPERATE
DELIVER
MANAGE

Why Use the Policy SMF?

This SMF provides sufficient context to understand the reasoning behind policies, the creation, validation and enforcement of policies, and how the policy management process communicates the policy and incorporates feedback about the policy. The purpose is to help the IT organization remain in compliance with directives. For the sake of clarity, these are the policies that address people and process; these are not machine-based control policies such as Group Policy Objects.

This SMF addresses how to:

- Determine areas requiring policy.
- Create policies.
- Validate policy.
- Publish policy.
- Enforce and evaluate policy.
- Review and maintain policy.

A policy explains what to do in a particular set of circumstances by providing necessary rules and requirements and by setting expectations about conduct. Policies help organizations clarify performance requirements, communicate management's intent for how work should be done, and establish accountability and the foundation for compliance. Although potentially wide-ranging, policy generally centers on the following topics:

- Policy governance
- Security
- Privacy
- Partner and third-party relationships
- Knowledge management
- Appropriate use

Goals of Policy

Successful policy management should result in documented, up-to-date guidelines that address the desired actions and behaviors of an organization. More specifically, it should ensure that:

- Policies accurately capture management's intent concerning the behaviors of the organization.
- Policies contain clear statements of rules, but their implementation is carried out through procedures and employee judgment.
- Policies are communicated consistently and effectively across the organization.
- Policies are defined in ways that take into account their eventual application and evaluation.

Table 4-6. Outcomes and Measures of the Policy SMF Goals

Outcomes	Measures
Policy supports management objectives	• Audits of policies indicate that they appropriately reflect management objectives.
Employees utilize policy	• There are no audit issues related to activities defined in policies.
Regulatory compliance	• All regulatory audits are passed with no deficiencies. For further information about regulatory compliance, see Understanding Regulatory Compliance on TechNet.
Organizational compliance	• All compliance audits are passed with no deficiencies (for example, security, privacy, or standards of conduct).

Policy Processes and Activities

Process 1: Determine Areas Requiring Policy

A key activity in Policy is the process of aligning the goals of the IT organization to those of the overall business, then using that information to decide which areas need to have policies created. Organizational goals should be evaluated to determine possible risks. The impact of risks can be evaluated by considering what might happen if the expectations surrounding that risk are not made clear to everyone in the organization. If an identified risk and its impact stand in the way of achieving a goal, then it will likely need to be addressed by a policy. In this way, management establishes clear guidelines that help ensure desired performance, f, and appropriate workplace interactions.

Activities include:

• Documenting goals.
• Assessing current state.

- Envisioning future state.
- Performing gap analysis.

Process 2: Create Policies

In this process, the group responsible for policy creation actually drafts the policies, often through the use of a standardized policy template. Specific types of policies are used to address different topic areas.

Activities include:
- Creating policy governance policies.
- Creating security policies.
- Creating privacy policies.
- Creating partner relationship policies.
- Creating knowledge management policies.
- Creating appropriate use policies

Process 3: Validate Policy

In this process, policies must be validated with all stakeholders of the business. Because an organization's policies may have serious legal implications, validation requires careful attention to detail.

Activities Include:
- Performing policy review.
- Reviewing comments and revising policies.
- Managing policy configuration.

Process 4: Publish Policy

In this process, policies are published for the organization to use. Although the process is fairly simple, the effects of poor publication can be difficult to recover from. The business must be notified in advance of the pending policy release, provided with the location of policies that everyone can find, and given the opportunity to become trained on the policies.

Process 5: Enforce and Evaluate Policy
In this process, policies are enforced, and then evaluated for their effectiveness. Without an evaluation exercise, organizations may find that certain policies are actually impeding people's ability to get work done; often an increase in the number and severity of violations is an indicator that policies need to be adjusted.

Activities include:
- Enforcing the policy.
- Requesting corrective action.
- Analyzing policy enforcement.
- Evaluating policy effectiveness.
- Requesting policy change.

Process 6: Review and Maintain Policy
Policies are only as effective as the relevance and accuracy of their information; policy violations increase when that information is out of date or doesn't address what the user is seeking. To ensure that policies stay current and relevant, the organization should schedule regular policy reviews and make adjustments and changes as a result of those reviews. Because policy change often has legal considerations, the process should include documentation indicating that changes have occurred, why they happened, and who approved them.

Activities include:
- Reviewing policy.
- Controlling policy configuration.
- Changing policy.

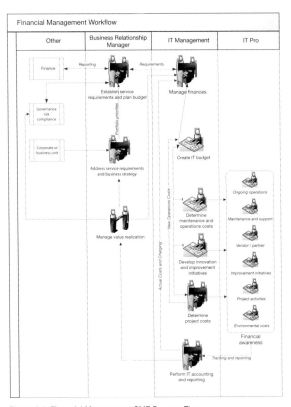

Figure 4-4. Financial Management SMF Process Flow

Financial Management SMF

- Business/IT Alignment
- Reliability
- Policy
- Financial Management ◄

Service Alignment

Portfolio

PLAN

MOF

OPERATE

DELIVER

MANAGE

Why Use the Financial Management SMF?

This SMF should be useful for anyone with responsibility for measuring and evaluating the costs and benefits—or more comprehensively, the business value—of IT services. It provides an understanding of the fundamental processes and activities involved and describes the context of financial management in terms of risk management and value realization.

It addresses how to do the following:

- Establish service requirements and plan budget.
- Manage finances.
- Perform IT accounting and reporting

When management makes decisions about changes to IT infrastructure, systems, staffing, or processes, it uses financial data to justify the cost. However, cost tells only part of the story; value must be considered as well. The concept of value reflects service levels, business impact, and both hard and soft benefits. Financial management ensures that IT services and solutions have agreed-upon value delivery expectations, as well as metrics for tracking and realizing value, cost justification, and adequate budgetary support.

Goals of Financial Management

Successful financial management will help an organization:

- Fully account for the cost of IT services while defining the expected contribution to the business.
- Attribute costs of services delivered to customers so that the costs can be recovered.
- Aid decision making by clarifying the costs, benefits, and risks of IT services.
- Contribute to business cases for changes to IT services based on a sound understanding of the cost-benefit tradeoffs involved.

The achievement of these objectives should result in several specific outcomes, which are detailed in the table below.

Table 4-7. Outcomes and Measures of the Financial Management SMF Goals

Outcomes	Measures
IT cost accounting	• IT costs accounted for and tracked • Costs reviewed and improvements in progress
Delivered business value	• Each project evaluated for expected business value • Project benefits consistently realized
IT cost recovery	• Customers charged fairly • Charging model relevant and appropriate for the organization
Accurate IT budget	• Comprehensive financial understanding within IT • Actual budget is close to projected budget, without surprises

Financial Management Processes and Activities

The following processes are included:

- Establish service requirements and plan budget.
- Manage finances.
- Perform IT accounting and reporting.

Process 1: Establish service requirements and plan budget

Proactive and strategic use of technology requires that IT departments do more than simply account for costs. IT must understand the broader drivers affecting the organization and translate these into IT service initiatives. When IT's expected contribution to business results is understood, these expected benefits need to be tracked and managed through a process called value realization.

Activities include:

- Addressing service requirements and business strategy.
- Planning a budget.
- Conducting a budget review.
- Managing IT value realization.

Process 2: Manage Finances

This process includes many traditional financial management activities, such as budgeting, costing models, charge-back models, cost allocations, cost management, and reporting. The process also involves preparing and managing an IT budget that reflects the business priorities identified earlier in the process. Most budgets are loosely categorized into three areas:

- Ongoing operations and maintenance spending (non-discretionary spending)
- Project spending (discretionary spending)

- Innovation—a focus on investments in improving the efficiency and effectiveness of ongoing operations and/or improvements to business value

Activities include:
- Managing IT finances.
- Creating IT budget.
- Determining maintenance and operations costs.
- Developing innovation and improvement initiatives.
- Determining project costs.
- Establishing value realization awareness across IT

Process 3: Perform IT Accounting and Reporting

The final process in the Financial Management SMF involves IT accounting, reporting, and cost recovery. The information recorded in this process provides financial managers with:
- Costs to use in budget comparisons.
- Service usage reports that can be used as the basis for cost recovery (if this is the model that the IT organization employs).
- The actual derived benefits to the business for the services that are delivered.

Value Realization

Value has multiple dimensions that vary from organization to organization. The value realization process quantifies the value of IT investments so that decision makers can prioritize according to expected value and, later, have the means to determine whether expected value was, in fact, realized.

Investment decisions should reflect three basic considerations:
- Invest only when value can be tied to organizational strategies.
- Invest only when the sponsor is willing to be held accountable.
- Invest only if value can be determined.

Investments yield value that can be separated into categories. Figure 4-5 shows some common ways to categorize value, along with examples of how a specific initiative should affect value in a number of different respects.

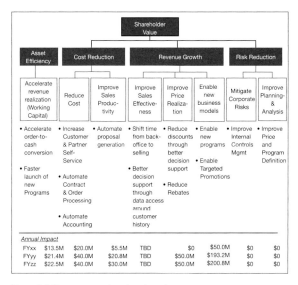

	Cost Reduction		Revenue Growth			Risk Reduction	
Asset Efficiency	**Cost Reduction**		**Revenue Growth**			**Risk Reduction**	
Accelerate revenue realization (Working Capital)	Reduce Cost	Improve Sales Produc-tivity	Improve Sales Effective-ness	Improve Price Realiza-tion	Enable new business models	Mitigate Corporate Risks	Improve Planning- & Analysis
• Accelerate order-to-cash conversion • Faster launch of new Programs	• Increase Customer & Partner Self-Service • Automate Contract & Order Processing • Automate Accounting	• Automate proposal generation	• Shift time from back-office to selling • Better decision support through data access around customer history	• Reduce discounts through better decision support • Reduce Rebates	• Enable new programs • Enable Targeted Promotions	• Improve Internal Controls Mgmt	• Improve Price and Program Definition

Annual Impact

FYxx $13.5M	$20.0M	$5.5M	TBD	$0	$50.0M	$0	$0
FYyy $21.4M	$40.0M	$20.8M	TBD	$50.0M	$193.2M	$0	$0
FYzz $22.5M	$40.0M	$30.0M	TBD	$50.0M	$200.8M	$0	$0

Figure 4-5. Common ways to categorize value.

Improving Planning in Your Organization

Use the following checklist to determine the right set of priorities for your organization. To support the right set of decisions, refer to the MOF guidance, which provides key questions, inputs, outputs and best practices that support decision making: www.microsoft.com/mof.

Business/IT Alignment SMF Checklist

- Define an IT service strategy.
- Identify and map services.
- Identify IT service demand and manage business requests.
- Develop and evaluate the IT service portfolio.
- Manage service levels.

Key Questions

- Is there an IT service strategy that is aligned to business goals and objectives?
- Are there service maps in place and are they up-to-date?
- Is IT service demand being measured and is there a process to manage new business requests and/or requirements?
- Is there a service portfolio in place and a process for evaluating new projects?
- Are you managing service levels with the use of service level agreements (SLA), operating level agreements (OLA) and underpinning contracts (UC)?

Reliability SMF Checklist

- Plan.
- Implement.
- Monitor and improve plans.

Key Questions

- Are there data confidentiality, data integrity, availability, disaster recovery, business continuity, and monitoring plans in place?
- Have the plans been implemented and integrated?
- Are the reliability requirements consistently monitored and are opportunities for improvement identified?

Policy SMF Checklist

- Determine areas requiring policy.
- Publish policy.
- Create policies.
- Enforce and evaluate policy.
- Validate policy.
- Review and manage policy.

Key Questions

- Is risk evaluated in determining which areas require policy?
- Are policies created around the following areas: security, privacy, appropriate use, partner relationship, governance policies, and knowledge management?
- Are policies validated to ensure they meet the correct criteria?
- Are all policies published in a manner where they are easily accessible by the appropriate parties?
- Are policies enforced and evaluated for effectiveness?
- Are policies reviewed to ensure they are at the right level?

Financial Management SMF Checklist

- Establish service requirements and plan budget.
- Manage finances.
- Perform IT accounting and reporting.

Key Questions

- Are service requirements clearly understood so an accurate budget is in place?
- Are finances managed according to commonly accepted accounting practices?
- Is there a method to demonstrate value creation and return on investment?

5. The Deliver Phase

Overview of the Deliver Phase

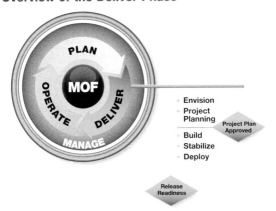

The Deliver Phase is where services are planned, designed, built, and deployed. This phase starts with an early form of planning called "envisioning," moves through a more formal project planning stage, continues with the build stage, follows up with testing, and ends with deployment. There are several choices that those managing a project can make in terms of a management discipline to apply to the project. Possibilities include Microsoft® Solutions Framework (MSF), agile software development, Capability Maturity Model Integration (CMMI) process management, Scrum, and Project Management Institute (PMI). While MSF is the basis for the SMFs in the Deliver Phase, organizations can easily adapt the information in those SMFs to any management discipline.

The Deliver Phase contains the following service management functions (SMFs): Envision, Project Planning, Build, Stabilize, and Deploy.

This phase is one in which project teams frequently play a major role. The primary team accountability that applies to the phase is the Solution Accountability, with the accountable role type for the phase being the Solution Manager, who has oversight for all solutions and their project teams.

Other key role types for the phase are Program Manager, Product Manager, and Developer. More information about those and other role types, as well as the Solutions Accountability to which they belong, can be found in the "Team SMF Focus" section of this document.

Goals of the Deliver Phase

The primary goals of the Deliver IT service lifecycle phase are to ensure that IT services, infrastructure projects, or packaged product deployments are envisioned, planned, built, stabilized, and deployed in line with business requirements and the customer's specifications.

Specifically, that means ensuring that the project team:
- Captures the business needs and requirements prior to planning a solution.
- Prepares a functional specification and solution design.
- Develops work plans, cost estimates, and schedules for the deliverables.
- Builds the solution to the customer's specification, so that all features are complete, and so that the solution is ready for external testing and stabilization.
- Releases the highest-quality solution by performing thorough testing and release-candidate piloting.
- Deploys a stable solution to the production environment and stabilizes the solution in production.
- Prepares the operations and support teams to manage and provide customer service for the solution.

Meeting these goals requires:

- Alignment with the service management functions (SMFs) for this phase.
- Using periodic management reviews (MRs) to evaluate the effectiveness of the phase.

SMFs, Management Reviews, and their Relationship in the Deliver Phase

Table 5-1. SMFs in the Deliver Phase

SMF	Deliverable/Purpose
Envision	**Deliverable:** Vision document **Purpose:** • Clearly communicate the project's vision, scope, and risk
Project Planning	**Deliverable:** Project plan document **Purpose:** • Obtain agreement from the project team, customer, and stakeholders that all interim milestones have been met, that the project plans reflect the customer's needs, and that the project plans are realistic
Build	**Deliverable:** Developed solution **Purpose:** • Build a solution that meets the customer's expectations and specifications as defined in the functional specification
Stabilize	**Deliverable:** Tested and stable solution **Purpose:** • Resolve all issues found by testing and through pilot feedback, and release a high-quality solution that meets the customer's expectations and specifications as defined in the functional specification
Deploy	**Deliverable:** Service in operation **Purpose:** • Deploy a stable solution that satisfies the customer, and successfully transfer it from the project team to the Operations and Support teams

Table 5-2. Management Reviews in the Deliver Phase

Management Reviews	Deliverable/Purpose
Project Plan Approved	**Deliverable:** A complete review and signoff of the project's functional specification, master plan, and master schedule. **Purpose:** • To clarify business requirements and to more precisely determine the level of effort and resources (people and funding) needed to complete the work.
Release Readiness	**Deliverable:** Review or assessment of the business' readiness to use the solution in its work. **Purpose:** • To confirm, or certify, release readiness.

Management Reviews

Project Plan Approved Management Review

After a project concept has been approved and a startup project team identified, work needs to be done to clarify business requirements and to more precisely determine the level of effort and resources (people and funding) needed to complete the work. At this point the team prepares the functional specification, works through the design process, and prepares work plans, cost estimates, and schedules for the various deliverables. The functional specification serves multiple purposes—it acts as:

• A set of instructions to developers about what to build

• A basis for estimating work

• An agreement with the customer about exactly what will be built

• A point of synchronization for the whole team

Release Readiness Management Review

The Release Readiness MR comes near the completion of the Deliver Phase, between Stabilize and Deploy. It represents a comprehensive review of the deliverables that were produced, as well as an assessment of the readiness of the business to employ this solution in its work and of IT operations and support readiness to take over responsibility for this solution in the production environment.

In this MR, a specially formed review team evaluates four distinct aspects of release readiness:

- The operability and supportability of the release itself
- The readiness of the production environment (organization and infrastructure) to support and operate the release
- The readiness of the business or customers to use new features and functionality
- The readiness of the release strategy plans, including rollout and rollback plans, training plans, and support plans

The purpose of the Release Readiness MR is to confirm, or certify, these items. Ready is defined as "meets business and IT needs and can support consistent, ongoing achievement of service level expectations."

Key Terms

Table 5-3. Key Terms

Term	Definition
Baseline	A known state by which something is measured or compared. Baselines make managing change in complex projects possible.
Bottom-up scheduling	Team members representing each role generate time estimates and schedules for deliverables. Each team's schedule is integrated into a master project schedule.
Conceptual design	Conceptual design involves understanding the business requirements and defining the features that users need to do their jobs. Product management takes the lead in creating the conceptual design, which begins during envisioning and continues with project planning.
Customer	The customer is the person or organization that commissions and funds the project.
Final release	The final, fully tested version of the solution. A final release is considered to be stable and relatively bug-free with a quality suitable for wide distribution and use by end users.
Functional testing	Testing a completed solution against the functional specification.
Integration testing	Testing individual, united tested components integrated with other components.
Milestone	A project synchronization point. Major milestones mark the transition of a project from one phase to the next phase. They also transfer primary responsibility from one role to another role. The Deliver Phase service management functions (SMFs) correspond to major Microsoft Solutions Framework (MSF) milestones.
Personas	Describes various types of users and their job functions, including operations staff.

Term	Definition
Physical design	Physical design describes the desired architecture in greater detail than the logical design. It also defines the hardware configurations and software products to be used. As a general rule, the design should contain enough detail to enable the team to begin work on the project plan.
Pilot test	Testing conducted by a subset of users in a production environment. The pilot group uses the solution, providing feedback and reporting any bugs the group finds.
Scope	A view of the project's vision limited by constraints such as time and resources. Solution scope describes the solution's features and deliverables. Project scope describes the work to be performed by the team.
Solution	A coordinated delivery of technologies, documentation, training, and support that successfully responds to a customer's business problem. Solutions typically combine people, processes, and technology to solve problems.
Stakeholder	Individuals or groups who have an interest in the outcome of the project. Their goals and priorities are not always identical to those of the customer. Examples of stakeholders include departmental managers who will be affected by the solution, IT staff who will be responsible for running and supporting the solution, and functional managers who contribute resources to the project team.
Unit testing	Testing individual solution components.
Use case	Describes an individual task performed in a use scenario.
Use scenario	Describes a particular activity that a user tries to accomplish, such as processing a transaction or checking e-mail.
Users	The people who interact with the solution to perform their jobs.
Vision	Describes the fundamental goals of the solution.

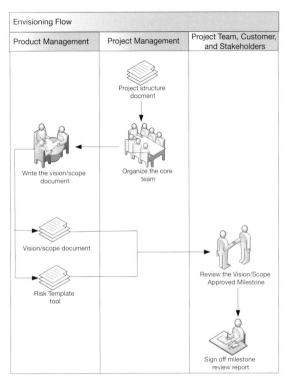

Figure 5-1. Envision SMF Process Flow

Envision SMF

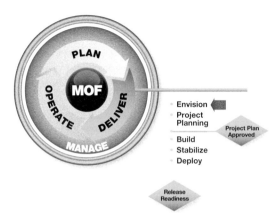

Envision ◄
Project
Planning

Project Plan
Approved

Build
Stabilize
Deploy

Release
Readiness

Why use the Envision SMF?

This SMF should be useful to anyone who is tasked with forming a core project team, preparing and delivering a vision/scope document that clearly communicates the project's vision and the scope of that vision, and preparing a risk assessment.

Goals of Envisioning

The primary goals of envisioning are to form the core project team, prepare and deliver a vision/scope document that clearly communicates the project's vision and the scope of that vision, and prepare a risk assessment. The following table shows the desired outcomes of the Envision SMF goals and lists measures that you can use to gauge how successfully you have achieved these goals after completing this SMF.

Table 5-4. Outcomes and Measures of the Envision SMF Goals

Outcomes	Measures
The vision and scope of the project are clearly documented and understood by the team and the customer.	• No miscommunications and misunderstandings are found later on in the project. • The vision and scope remain largely intact throughout the project. • The vision/scope document is approved by the team and stakeholders. • Signoff on the Vision/Scope Approved Milestone occurs.
The project's risks are clearly documented and understood by the team and the customer.	• No unaddressed issues occur during the project. • Risk assessment is approved by the team and stakeholders. • Signoff on the Vision/Scope Approved Milestone occurs.

Envision Processes and Activities

Process 1: Organize the Core Team

During this process, management assigns core members to the project team. Typically, management does not assemble the full team yet. The initial team often plays multiple roles until all members are in place.

After assigning the core team, management creates a project structure document that describes the team's organization and the roles and specific responsibilities assigned to each team member. The project structure document also clarifies the chain of accountability to the customer and specifies the designated points of contact that the project team has with the customer. These can vary depending on the circumstances of the project.

Process 2: Write the Vision/Scope Document

During this process, the project team completes the first draft of the vision/scope document and distributes it to the team, customers, and stakeholders for review. During the review process, the document undergoes multiple iterations of feedback, discussion, and change.

The vision/scope provides clear direction for the project team; outlines explicit project goals, priorities, and constraints; and sets customer expectations.

Project vision and project scope are distinct concepts, and successful projects require both. Project vision is an unlimited view of the solution. Project scope identifies the parts of the vision that a project team can accomplish within its constraints. The vision/scope document defines both concepts.

Another key activity of this process is for the team to assess and document the project risks. This is done using the Risk Template.

Process 3: Approve the Vision/Scope Document

Finally, the project team obtains signoff from the customer and the stakeholders and then completes the milestone review report.

During this process, the team completes the milestone review report for the Vision/Scope Approved Milestone. The team, customers, and stakeholders sign off on this report to indicate their approval of the vision/scope document. Signoff also indicates that the team, customers, and stakeholders agree that the project team has met the requirements for completing the Vision/Scope Approved Milestone and that the project is ready to proceed to planning.

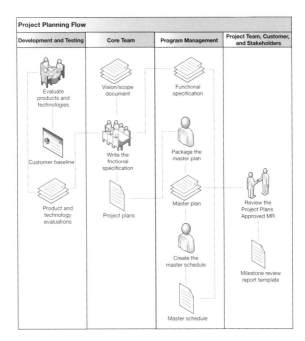

Project Planning Flow			
Development and Testing	**Core Team**	**Program Management**	**Project Team, Customer, and Stakeholders**

- Evaluate products and technologies
- Customer baseline
- Product and technology evaluations
- Vision/scope document
- Write the fnctional specification
- Project plans
- Functional specification
- Package the master plan
- Master plan
- Create the master schedule
- Master schedule
- Review the Project Plans Approved MR
- Milestone review report template

Figure 5-2. Project Planning SMF Process Flow

Project Planning SMF

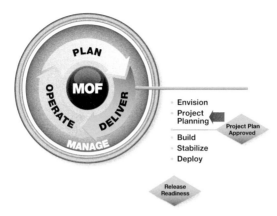

Why use the Project Planning SMF?

The Project Planning SMF should be useful to anyone who has the primary role in planning an IT service project, including preparing the functional specification and solution design and preparing work plans, cost estimates, and schedules.

Goals of Project Planning

The ultimate goal of project planning is to deliver a clearly scoped plan for building and delivering an IT service solution, which is represented by a master project plan, a master project schedule, and a functional specification at the Project Plans Approved MR, when the project team, its customers, and its stakeholders agree that the team has met all interim milestones.

Project Planning Processes and Activities
Process 1: Evaluate Products and Technologies

During this process, the project team evaluates products and technologies that it is considering using for building or deploying the

Table 5-5. Outcomes and Measures of the Project Planning SMF Goals

Outcomes	Measures
The design and features of the solution are clearly documented in the functional specification	• Number of bugs filed during development • Number of change requests needed for clarification • Functional specification approved by the team and stakeholders • Signoff on the Project Plans Approved MR • Support tickets during pilot or other phases of the project
The design and features of the solution are clearly traceable to business, user, operational, and system requirements	• Number of features that cannot be traced to requirements • Functional specification approved by the team and stakeholders • Signoff on the Project Plans Approved MR
The project plans clearly describe the tasks for which the project team is responsible and the schedules for performing those tasks	• Number of tasks completed on schedule and as planned • Master project plan approved by the team and stakeholders • Master project schedule approved by the team and stakeholders • Signoff on the Project Plans Approved MR

solution. The team members with the Development and Test roles perform the evaluation to ensure that the products and technologies under consideration work according to the vendor's specifications and meet the project's requirements. This effort eventually produces a proof of concept and ultimately evolves into the development of the solution.

Process 2: Write the Functional Specification
At the beginning of this process, the project team analyzes and creates the requirements documents. There are four categories of requirements: business, user, operational, and system.

The team then uses the requirements documents, a use scenarios document, and the product and technology evaluations from the previous process to develop a functional specification that it submits to its customer and stakeholders for review.

The project team also creates the design documents that record the results of the design process. These documents are separate from the functional specification and are focused on describing the internal workings of the solution.

Process 3: Package the Master Project Plan

After the team baselines the functional specification, it can begin detailed planning. The team leads prepare project plans for the deliverables in their areas of responsibility and participate in team planning sessions. As a group, the team reviews and identifies dependencies among the plans they have created.

The master project plan, then, is the collection of the individual project plans that allows for concurrent planning by various team roles and provides for clear accountability because specific roles are responsible for specific plans. It facilitates synchronization into a single schedule, facilitates reviews and approvals, and helps to identify gaps and inconsistencies.

Process 4: Create the Master Schedule

The master schedule includes all of the detailed project schedules, including the release date for the solution. Like the master project plan, the master schedule combines and integrates all the schedules from each team lead (bottom-up estimating). The team determines the release date after creating drafts of the functional specification and master project plan.

Process 5: Review the Project Plans Approved Milestone

In this final process, the project team, customers, and stakeholders sign off the milestone review report for the Project Plans Approved Milestone, which is also a MOF Management Review.

Building Flow

Development and Testing	Release Management	Project Team, Customer, and Stakeholders

Prepare for development

Functional specification

Prepare for release

Develop the solution

Deployment and training material

Solution

Sign off the milestone review report for the Scope Complete Milestone

Milestone review report document

Build SMF

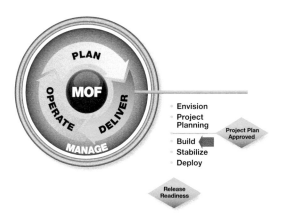

Why use the Build SMF?

This SMF should be useful for anyone who is involved with a project team tasked with the actual development of an IT service solution, with creating a development and test lab, or with preparing an IT service solution for pilot deployment.

Goals of Building

The primary goals of the building process are to develop the solution deliverables to the customer's specifications, develop the solution documentation, create the development and test lab, and prepare the solution for pilot deployment.

The Developer role type is primarily responsible for this goal, but all roles participate in building the solution. To achieve this goal, Development provides low-level solution and feature design, estimates the effort to deliver that design, and builds the solution. Additionally, Development serves the entire team as

Table 5-6. Outcomes and Measures of the Build SMF Goals

Outcomes	Measures
A solution delivered to the customer that is free of defects	• Number of bugs unresolved or deferred • Signoff on the Scope Complete Milestone
A solution that meets the customer's specifications as described in the functional specification	• Number of design change requests filed • Number of bugs filed for incorrect implementation • Signoff on the Scope Complete Milestone
A solution delivered to the customer within the schedule's specified timeline	• Date the Scope Complete Milestone is approved

technology consultant, validating technical decisions and mitigating development risks.

Build Processes and Activities

Process 1: Prepare for Development

Development begins with preparation. The project team needs to set up a development and test lab, create issue-tracking procedures, and begin test preparations.

The team should also prepare procedures for tracking issues and their resolutions. Not only do these procedures provide tracking and status information, they also contain information that operations and support will find invaluable after deploying the solution.

After the lab and issue-tracking procedures are in place, the team can begin test preparations: This includes reviewing the functional specification, preparing test cases, and preparing test scenarios.

Process 2: Develop the Solution

In this process, Development develops the solution, User Experience writes the documentation, and Test reviews the builds.

Because the development process focuses on developing the solution, the project needs interim milestones that can help the team measure build progress. The development of the solution's components is done in parallel and in segments, so the team needs a way to measure progress as a whole. Internal builds accomplish this by forcing the team to synchronize components at a solution level.

Process 3: Prepare for Release

During the release preparation process, the team begins developing content and procedures for deploying the solution into the production environment. The first activity is to create deployment content. This includes updating the master plan, including the deployment plan. The second activity is to begin developing training content for the users who will interact with the solution and for IT staff members who will deploy, operate, and support the solution.

Process 4: Review the Scope Complete Milestone

To complete this process, the project team, customers, and stakeholders review the Scope Complete Milestone. They agree that the team has met all interim milestones and that the full scope of the solution as defined in the functional specification has been developed. After reviewing and approving the Scope Complete Milestone, the project team is ready to move on to stabilizing.

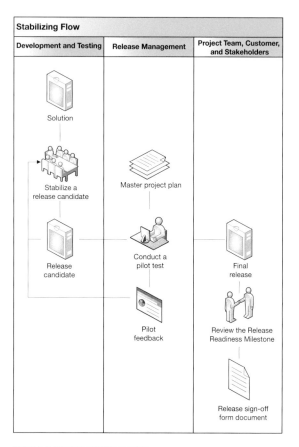

Stabilizing Flow		
Development and Testing	Release Management	Project Team, Customer, and Stakeholders

Solution

Stabilize a release candidate

Master project plan

Release candidate

Conduct a pilot test

Final release

Pilot feedback

Review the Release Readiness Milestone

Release sign-off form document

Figure 5-4. Stabilize SMF Process Flow

Stabilize SMF

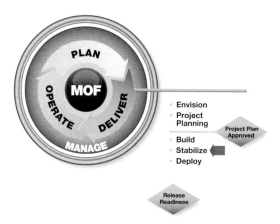

Why use the Stabilize SMF?

This SMF should be useful to anyone who is tasked with ensuring the release of the highest-quality IT service solution possible at the Release Readiness Milestone. It includes guidance for how to test a feature-complete solution, prepare release candidate versions, deal with feedback, and fix reported issues.

The SMF specifically addresses the following processes for stabilization:

- Stabilize a release candidate.
- Conduct a pilot test.
- Review the Release Readiness Management Review.

Goals of Stabilizing

The goal of stabilizing is to release the highest-quality solution possible at the Release Readiness Milestone. The project team achieves this goal by identifying bugs and issues through thorough testing and release-candidate piloting. Then, the team triages and resolves all known bugs. Resolving a bug doesn't exactly mean fixing it—it can be deferred to a later version or declared not serious enough to fix.

Table 5-7. Outcomes and Measures of the Stabilize SMF Goals

Outcomes	Measures
A high-quality, stable solution	• Bug convergence and zero bug bounce achieved • No unresolved bugs in the issue-tracking database
All issues found by testing and through pilot feedback are resolved	• The number of unresolved bugs in the issue-tracking database • Signoff on the Release Readiness Milestone
A high-quality solution that meets the customer's expectations and specifications as defined in the functional specification	• Signoff on the Release Readiness Milestone

Stabilize Processes and Activities

Process 1: Stabilize a Release Candidate

The first process in stabilizing is for the team to find and resolve bugs in the solution and to prepare a release candidate.

During the initial parts of stabilizing, Test and Development work together to find and resolve bugs. They hold regularly scheduled bug meetings to triage bugs, and team members report and track the status of each issue by using the issue-tracking procedures developed during planning.

As the project progresses, the team begins to prepare release candidates. Building a release candidate involves ensuring its fitness for release, including whether all of the components are present. Typically, teams will create multiple release candidates with each release candidate being an interim milestone. Testing after each release candidate indicates whether the candidate is fit to deploy to a pilot group.

Process 2: Conduct a Pilot Test

A pilot test verifies that the solution meets the expectations and specifications of the customer by testing the entire solution in a production environment. During the pilot test, the team collects and evaluates pilot data, such as user feedback. Once the team has collected enough data, the team must choose one of the following strategies:

- **Stagger forward.** Deploy a new release candidate to the pilot group.
- **Roll back.** Execute the rollback plan to restore the pilot group to its previous configuration state. Try the pilot again later with a more stable release candidate.
- **Suspend.** Suspend pilot testing.
- **Patch and continue.** Deploy patches to fix the existing solution.
- **Deploy.** Proceed to deployment of the solution.

Process 3: Review the Release Readiness Milestone

Stabilizing culminates in the Release Readiness Milestone. This milestone, which is a MOF Management Review, occurs after a successful pilot has been conducted, all outstanding issues have been addressed, and the solution is released and made available for full deployment in the production environment. This milestone is the opportunity for customers and users, operations and support personnel, and key project stakeholders to evaluate the solution and identify any remaining issues that they must address before deployment.

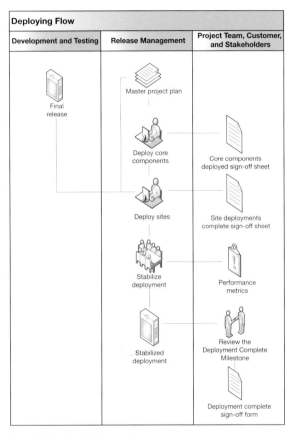

Deploying Flow		
Development and Testing	**Release Management**	**Project Team, Customer, and Stakeholders**

Master project plan

Final release

Deploy core components

Core components deployed sign-off sheet

Deploy sites

Site deployments complete sign-off sheet

Stabilize deployment

Performance metrics

Stabilized deployment

Review the Deployment Complete Milestone

Deployment complete sign-off form

Figure 5-5. Deploy SMF Process Flow

Deploy SMF

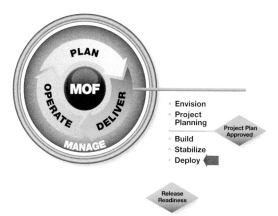

Why use the Deploy SMF?

This SMF should be useful for anyone who is involved with releasing a stable IT service solution into the production environment, including stabilizing the solution in the production environment and transferring responsibility for the solution from the project team to the Operations and Support teams.

It addresses how to do the following:

- Deploy core IT service solution components.
- Deploy sites.
- Stabilize deployment.
- Review the Deployment Complete Milestone.

Goal of Deployment

Deployment includes stabilizing the solution in the production environment and transferring responsibility for the solution from the project team to the operations and support teams. The table below shows the desired outcomes of the Deploy SMF goals and lists

Table 5-8. Outcomes and Measures of the Deploy SMF Goal

Outcomes	Measures
Stable solution deployed to the production environment	• Number of support issues opened post deployment
Customer is satisfied with and accepts the deployed solution	• All sites are fully deployed • Signoff on the Deployment Complete Milestone
Solution successfully transferred from the project team to the operations and support teams	• No project team members still actively involved in the project • Number of support escalations from operations and support teams

measures that you can use to gauge how successfully you have achieved these goals after completing this SMF.

Deploy Processes and Activities

Process 1: Deploy Core Components

IT solutions usually require supporting infrastructure in which to deploy and operate. Infrastructure examples include domain controllers, e-mail servers, remote access servers, and database servers. Although users don't interact directly with the infrastructure, the solution usually depends on it. Project teams can deploy the core technology before or in parallel with the solution, depending on the solution's requirements.

Process 2: Deploy Sites

This process is the ultimate goal of all of the project's previous processes. During this process, the project team deploys the solution to all targeted users and computers at each site. Customer and user feedback from the deployed sites may reveal additional problems with the solution. Therefore, the project team may have to revisit some sites after deployment. Still, the project team is making a concentrated effort to complete deployment and close the project. At the completion of this process, all targeted users and computers have access to the solution. Additionally, each site owner has signed off that their site is operating as expected.

Process 3: Stabilize Deployment

At the completion of this process, the customer and the project team agree that site deployments are complete and that they are operating satisfactorily. This means that the solution and the site deployments are meeting customer expectations and specifications and that the customer is willing to approve and sign off on them.

Determining when a project is complete and the project team can disengage can be difficult. New solutions are often constantly changing, and the project team is often fire-fighting—identifying and managing support issues. Even though the project team might find it difficult to formally close the project because of ongoing issues, the team needs to clearly define a completion milestone and completion criteria.

Process 4: Review the Deployment Complete Milestone

The Deployment Complete Milestone finalizes the project and signifies that the project team has fully disengaged and transferred the solution to permanent personnel. At the completion of this milestone, the project team signs off on the milestone review report document to signify their approval of the milestone. Additionally, the project team, customers, and stakeholders complete the post-project analysis document and the project close-out report to document lessons learned and best practices.

Improving Delivery in Your Organization

Use the following checklist to determine the right set of priorities for your organization. To support the right set of decisions, refer to the MOF guidance, which provides key questions, inputs, outputs and best practices that support decision making: www.microsoft.com/mof.

Envision SMF Checklist
- Organize the core project team.
- Approve the vision/scope document.
- Write the vision/scope document.

Key Questions
- Have you identified possible core project team members that can also play multiple roles?
- Have you written the vision / scope document at a strategic level of detail?
- Do you have a milestone review report that has been approved by the team, customers and stakeholders?

Project Planning SMF Checklist
- Evaluate products and technologies.
- Write the functional specification.
- Package the master project plan.
- Create the master schedule.
- Review the Project Plans Approved Milestone

Key Questions
- Are your chosen products and technologies working based on the vendors' specifications and project requirements?
- Did you map the items in the functional specification to the requirement IDs?

- Have you incorporated all of the relevant project plans into the master project plan?
- Did you include the release date for the solution in the master schedule?
- Have you made sure that all the due dates for the interim milestones are realistic and that the roles and responsibilities are well defined?

Build SMF Checklist
- Prepare for development.
- Develop the solution.
- Prepare for release.
- Review the Scope Complete Milestone and sign off the milestone review report.

Key Questions
- To ensure an environment conducive to development, do you have a development lab available?
- Are you using internal builds as a way of measuring progress when developing solutions?
- Are you developing deployment and training content in preparation for the release of the solution?
- Did the project team, customers, and stakeholders review the Scope Complete Milestone?

Stabilize SMF Checklist
- Stabilize a release candidate.
- Conduct a pilot test.
- Review the Release Readiness Milestone.

Key Questions
- Did you allow the stakeholders to interact with the solution in the development environment prior to deploying a release candidate?

- Have you collected enough data during the pilot test to support the strategy you will choose?
- Are the customers and users, operations and support personnel, and key project stakeholders going to evaluate the solution to identify any remaining issues prior to deployment?
- Are the stakeholders ready for the release?

Deploy SMF Checklist
- Deploy core IT service solution components.
- Deploy sites.
- Stabilize deployment.
- Review the Deployment Complete Milestone.

Key Questions
- What infrastructure is needed for the solution, and has it been deployed properly based on the solution's requirements?
- Were additional problems with the solution revealed during deployment to the sites?
- Do you have a clearly defined completion milestone that will mark that site deployment is complete?
- Did the project team, customers, and stakeholders complete the post-project analysis document and project close-out report?

6. The Operate Phase

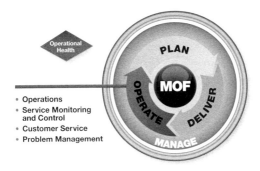

- Operations
- Service Monitoring and Control
- Customer Service
- Problem Management

Overview of the Operate Phase

The Operate Phase of the IT service lifecycle represents the culmination of the two phases that precede it. It contains the following service management functions (SMFs): Operations, Service Monitoring and Control, Customer Service, and Problem Management.

This phase is characterized mostly by dedicated teams, which are teams that exists for ongoing work, with no specific end time in mind. The role types on those teams fall into two accountabilities: the Operations Accountability and the Support Accountability. The accountable role type for the Operations Accountability is the Operations Manager. The accountable role type for the Support Accountability is the Customer Service Manager.

The Operate Phase begins after a new service has been deployed in the Deliver Phase. The end of the Deliver phase is tied to the Release Readiness Management Review (MR), which occurs between Stabilize and Deploy. This review, and the post-implementation review that occurs after deployment is complete, acts as a bridge between the Deliver Phase and the Operate Phase, ensuring the readiness of the release for deployment, including the operability and supportability of the release and the readiness of the target production environment to support and operate the deployed release.

In turn, the Operate Phase is supported by a management review, the Operational Health Review (OHR), which includes a review of service level agreements (SLAs) and operating level agreements (OLAs). The Operational Health Review should be scheduled on a regular basis to ensure that operations in the production environment are continuously monitored and measured against previously set indicators. This review evaluates performance-related metrics, as well as other business and operational indicators that help measure the overall health of the production computing environment.

Goals of the Operate Phase
The primary goals of the Operate Phase are to ensure that deployed services are operated, monitored, and supported in line with the agreed-to SLA targets.

Specifically, that means:
- Ensuring that IT services are available by improving IT staff use and better managing workload.
- Ensuring that IT services are monitored to provide real-time observation of health conditions and by ensuring that team members are trained to handle any problems efficiently and quickly.
- Ensuring that IT services are restored quickly and effectively.

Meeting these goals requires:
- Alignment with the service management functions (SMFs) for this phase.
- Using periodic management reviews (MRs) to evaluate the effectiveness of the phase.

SMFs, Management Reviews, and their Relationship in the Operate Phase

Table 6-1. SMFs in the Operate Phase

SMF	Deliverable/Purpose
Operations	**Deliverable:** Operations guide **Purpose:** • Ensure that the work required to successfully operate IT services has been identified and described • Free up time for the operations staff by reducing reactive work • Minimize service disruptions and downtime • Execute recurring IT operations work effectively and efficiently
Service Monitoring and Control	**Deliverable:** IT health monitoring data **Purpose:** • Observe the health of IT services • Initiate remedial actions to minimize the impact of service incidents and system events
Customer Service	**Deliverable:** Effective user service **Purpose:** • Provide a positive experience to the users of a service provider • Address complaints or issues
Problem Management	**Deliverable:** Effective problem resolution process **Purpose:** • Provide root cause analysis to identify problems • Predict future problems

Table 6-2. Management Reviews in the Operate Phase

Management Reviews	Deliverable/Purpose
Operational Health Review	**Deliverable:** Operational health review **Purpose:** • to ensure that operations in the production environment are continuously monitored and measured against previously set indicators.

Management Review for the Phase

The MR for the Operate Phase is a periodic review that is key to the effective maintenance, monitoring, and support of IT services, as well the actions taken to improve them. That review—the Operational Health Review—provides a structure for reviewing and analyzing results and taking action to improve performance. It takes place at the end of the Operate Phase and is primarily concerned with assessing the effectiveness of an organization's internal operating processes. It is intended to be scheduled on a regular basis, but may be called into session on an emergency basis. The goal is to ensure that operations in the production environment are continuously monitored and measured against previously set indicators.

Items to evaluate:

- OLA-defined targets and metrics
- SLA-defined targets and metrics
- Contractual targets and metrics
- Customer satisfaction
- Costs
- IT staff performance
- Operational efficiency
- Personnel skills and competencies

The key stakeholders and decision makers who participate in the OHR meeting include:

- The IT operations management team.
- The service managers responsible for the services being delivered.
- Managers from platform or technology-specific teams (such as network administration, messaging, data lifecycle management).
- Event monitoring team (also known as bridge or command center).
- Storage management, backup, and recovery team.
- Security administration team.
- Delivery representation (development, test).
- Customer representation.
- User representation.
- Partner representation.

Key Terms

Table 6-3. Key Terms

Term	Definition
Aggregation	A function that makes it possible to treat a series of similar events as a single event
Alert	A notification that an event requiring attention has occurred
Configuration item (CI)	An IT component that is under configuration management control
Configuration management system	A set of tools used to manage IT service management data such as changes, releases, known errors, and incidents
Correlation	A function that groups events together or defines an event's relationship with other events that together represent an impact
Customer Service Representative (CSR)	A front-line contact person on the Service Desk team
Error	A fault, bug, or behavior issue in an IT service or system
Event	An occurrence within the IT environment detected by a monitoring tool
Health model	A definition of CI health categorized by availability, configuration, performance, or security
Incident	Failure of a service or component to provide a feature it was designed to deliver
Incident resolution request	An inquiry to resolve the failure of a service or feature
Information request	An inquiry to gain additional information about an existing service. This does not include activating new features or providing new services
IT Control	A specific activity performed by people or systems designed to ensure that business objectives are met

Term	Definition
Known error	An error that has been observed and documented
Known error database	A subsection of the knowledge base or overall configuration management system (CMS) that stores known errors and their associated root causes, workarounds, and fixes
New service request	An inquiry to gain a new service or feature
Operations guide	An operations plan containing prescriptive work instructions
Operations log	Records listing when operational work has been completed and by whom
Problem	A scenario describing symptoms that have occurred in an IT service or system that threatens its availability or reliability
Reporting	The collection, production, and distribution of information about IT services
Root cause	The specific reason that most directly contributes to the occurrence of an error
Rules	A predetermined policy that describes the provider (the source of data), the criteria (used to identify a matching condition), and the response (the execution of an action)
Service	A collection of features and functions that enable a business process
Service window	The Span of time during which maintenance of an IT service can be completed without affecting the availability specified in the SLA
Threshold/criteria	A configurable value above which something is true and below which it is not

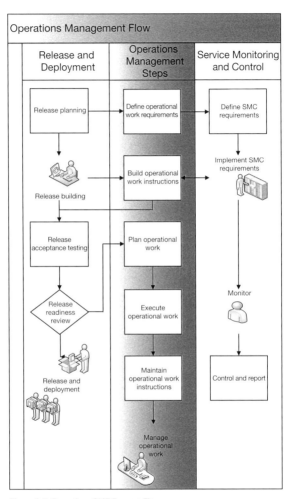

Figure 6-1. Operations SMF Process Flow

Operations SMF

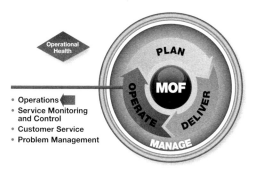

- Operations
- Service Monitoring and Control
- Customer Service
- Problem Management

Why Use the Operations SMF?

This SMF should be useful to anyone who is tasked with ensuring effective day-to-day operations, including ensuring that required work is identified, reactive time spent is reduced, disruptions are minimized, and recurring tasks are executed well.

This SMF specifically addresses how to:

- Define operational work requirements.
- Build operational work instructions.
- Plan operational work.
- Execute operational work.
- Maintain operational work instructions.
- Manage operational work.

Goals of Operations

The goals of Operations include the following:

- Ensure that the work required to successfully operate IT services has been identified and described.
- Reduce time spent by Operations staff on reactive work.
- Minimize service disruptions and downtime.

- Execute recurring and on-demand IT operations tasks effectively and efficiently.

Table 6-4. Outcomes and Measures of the Operations SMF Goals

Outcomes	Measures
Improve efficiency of IT staff	• Number of Operations staff, number of work hours used outside operations plan
Increase IT service availability	• Service availability, service level agreement (SLA) targets missed
Improved operations of new/ changed IT services	• Number of incidents the first month
Reduction of reactive work	• Reduction in number of incidents

Operations Processes and Activities

Process 1: Define Operational Work Requirements

The objective of this process is to identify and document the work activities that ensure optimal IT operation.

With the help of the Technology Area Manager, the release team:
- Identifies the operational requirements imposed by SLAs and operating level agreements (OLAs).
- Categorizes typical operational activities and tasks.
- Builds an operations plan that details those items, as well as their requirements and dependencies.

Process 2: Build Operational Work Instructions

The objective of this process is to develop guidance and specific, tested instructions for the operational work identified in the operations plan. This includes:
- Identifying resources.
- Developing operational work instructions.
- Identifying operational guidance.
- Testing operational work instructions.

Process 3: Plan Operational Work

This process includes:

- Categorizing operational work.
- Assigning resources.
- Estimating duration.
- Identifying dependencies.
- Building the operations schedule.

Process 4: Execute Operational Work

This process helps guarantee that the work specified in the operations guide is executed according to the operations schedule effectively, efficiently, and with predictable results. It is also essential that knowledge gathered while performing the operational work is captured and used to continually improve the quality of service delivery.

This process includes:

- Executing work instructions.
- Updating operations log.
- Supplying input for ORM.

Process 5: Maintain Operational Work Instructions

The objective of this process is to change or retire existing work instructions. Generally, work instructions change because a better way of completing the work has been identified. Work instructions are retired when the service they address is retired or otherwise becomes obsolete.

This process includes:

- Performing maintenance.
- Updating the operations guide.

Process 6: Manage Operational Work

In this process, the Operations Manager ensures that work outlined in the operations guide is completed cost-effectively and is fulfilling the SLAs. Additionally, IT staff members document relevant experiences for future reference, which helps reduce both the number of incidents and the amount of unplanned work.

This process includes:
- Verifying work completed.
- Optimizing operations resources.
- Optimizing the operations schedule

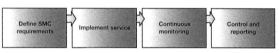

Figure 6-2. Service Monitoring and Control SMF Process Flow
Note: The detailed process flow can be found in the MOF 4.0 Guidance at
www.microsoft.com/mof

Service Monitoring and Control (SMC) SMF

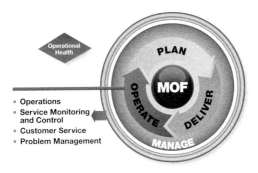

- Operations
- Service Monitoring and Control
- Customer Service
- Problem Management

Why use the SMC SMF?

This SMF should be useful to anyone who is responsible for the real-time observation of and alerting about conditions in an IT production environment.

It specifically addresses how to:

- Define service monitoring requirements.
- Implement a service.
- Conduct continuous monitoring.

Goals of SMC

The goals of service monitoring and control include the following:

- Observe the health of IT services.
- Take remedial actions that minimize the impact of service incidents and system events.
- Understand the infrastructure components responsible for the delivery of services.
- Provide data on component or service trends that can be used to optimize the performance of IT services.

The achievement of these goals should result in several specific, measurable outcomes, which are detailed in the table below.

Table 6-5. Outcomes and Measures of the SMC SMF Goals

Outcomes	Measures
Improved overall availability of services	• Percent of time service is available
A reduction in the number of SLA and OLA breaches	• Number of breaches to SLAs and OLAs
A reduction or prevention of service incidents through the use of proactive remedial action	• Number of service incidents

SMC Processes and Activities

Process 1: Define Service Monitoring Requirements

Before introducing a new service into the IT environment, the SMC team needs to determine what is required to monitor the health of the service. The SMC team works with those who will release the new service and those responsible for ongoing operations of the service after its release to the production environment to identify needs and dependencies, breaking down the service into steps to ensure accurate monitoring. This information is used to create a health model, which defines whether a system is healthy—that is, operating within normal conditions—or if it has somehow failed or degraded. This model becomes the basis for system events and instrumentation on which monitoring and automated recovery are built.

This process includes the following activities:

• Define the IT service to be monitored.
• Prepare the service component health model.
• Review the reliability requirements.

Process 2: Implement New Service

Successfully implementing a new service requires ensuring that it aligns with what is already in place. The first activity ensures that the new service meshes with existing IT processes and functions; the second concerns the service's impact on the people within IT. Finally, the third activity brings the service in line with existing IT tools and processes.

Implementing a new service involves the following activities:
- Align new IT service to existing processes and functions.
- Align new IT service to existing IT organization.
- Align the new IT service to existing SMC tools.

Process 3: Continuous Monitoring

The third process in SMC occurs after any monitoring tool being used is in place. When an event occurs, a notification is received, either by a dedicated SMC group or by a related group that has SMC responsibilities. After analysis, the event is either solved or escalated to a higher level for eventual solution.

This process involves the following activities:
- Receive notification.
- Analyze the event.
- Solve or escalate the event.

Process 4: Control and Reporting

The fourth SMC process, Control and Reporting, involves generating information for the entire IT organization and ensuring that ongoing monitoring is doing its intended job.

This process consists of the following activities:
- Produce reports and statistics.
- Conduct Operational Health management review (MR).
- Plan and execute service improvements.

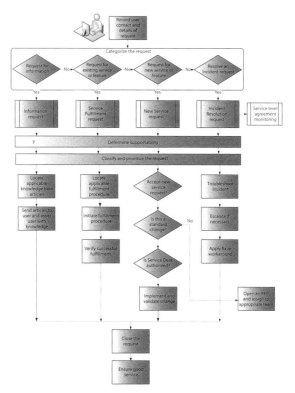

Figure 6-3. Customer Service SMF Process Flow

Customer Service SMF

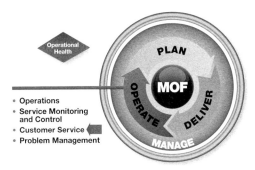

- Operations
- Service Monitoring and Control
- Customer Service
- Problem Management

Why Use the Customer Service SMF?

This SMF should be useful to anyone who is involved in providing a positive experience for IT service users by meeting their IT needs and addressing complaints and issues that arise during the normal course of using an IT service.

It addresses how to provide that experience by:

- Recording and determining the nature of a customer request.
- Resolving requests for information, for existing and new features, and for changes.
- Resolving incidents.
- Ensuring good customer service.

Goals of Customer Service

The driving vision for the Service Desk is to translate the complexities of IT into a one-stop shop for IT users. The process flow defined in the Customer Service SMF provides the Service Desk with the guidance it needs to achieve its vision in an efficient, cost-effective way. The table below shows the desired outcomes of the Customer Service SMF goals and lists measures that you can use to gauge how successfully you have achieved these goals.

Table 6-6. Outcomes and Measures of the Customer Service SMF Goals

Outcomes	Measures
Maintain business productivity	• Restore services or service features to a satisfactory operational state • Provide guidance and "how to" information
Increase value added by IT	• Facilitate Service Fulfillment requests • Improve user satisfaction
Improve business functionality, competitiveness, and efficiency	• Assess requests for new services and features for potential fulfillment by existing services • Filter out insufficient justification for new services and features

Customer Service Processes and Activities

Process 1: Record the User's Request

When a user contacts the Service Desk, the first step that the customer service representative (CSR) must take is to open a Help request, and then perform the following tasks:

• Record the user's contact information.
• Record the details of the user's situation.

Only when this information has been documented can the CSR move on to the next process—categorizing the user's request.

Process 1a: Record the User's Contact Information

The first step in keeping accurate records is to open a Help request for every user call and record the user's contact information. Help requests can also be opened automatically by input generated from a system alert or from a user through a self-service portal, a link embedded in an application or Web site, or e-mail. Automated inputs are scripted to open Help requests and record data. Manual inputs include direct phone calls and instant messages. These create real-time connections between users and CSRs, as well as requiring CSRs to manually open Help requests to capture the contact.

The activities involved in recording the user's contact information include:

- Opening a Help request and recording the user's contact information.
- Receiving an automated Help request generated by a system alert.
- Receiving an automated Help request generated by a user-initiated request from a link in an application or a Web site, or from a self-service portal.

Process 1b: Record Details of the User's Request
Once the CSR has collected the basic user contact information, the next process is to record some details of the user's request. This information ensures that critical information is captured up front so that in the event that the user is disconnected from the CSR, he or she does not have to repeat the details.

The activities involved in recording the details of the user's request include:

- Recording the details of the user's request.
- Validating the data contained in an automated Help request.

Process 2: Classify the User's Request
After obtaining the user's contact information and some details of the user's request, the next process is for the CSR to determine what type of request the user needs assistance with by performing the following tasks:

- Categorize the user's request. This helps the CSR determine which solution will best benefit the user.
- Determine if the request is supportable.
- Prioritize the request.

Process 2a: Categorize the User's Request

Categorizing the user's request allows the CSR to identify the solution that will best benefit the user. The activities involved in categorizing the user's request include determining:

- If this is an Information request.
- If this is a request for an existing service or feature.
- If this is a request for a new service or feature
- If this request concerns a failure with an existing service or feature.

Process 2b: Determine Supportability

The second process in categorizing a request is to determine its supportability. Answering the fundamental question, "*Do we support this?*" is a common problem for support teams.

The activities involved in determining supportability include:

- Determining if this is a supported service.
- Determining whether to override an unsupported request if this is not a supported service.

Process 2c: Prioritize the Request

A key success factor in reducing the time required to resolve a request is the ability to match requests against known errors, workarounds, and knowledge base articles. This can only be effective if requests are consistently classified using predetermined metadata.

The activities involved in prioritizing the request include:

- Determining the impact and urgency of the request.
- Prioritizing the importance of the request.

Process 3: Resolve the Request

The path to resolving a request is different depending on the category of the request. The categories are:

- **Information request**. This is usually a request for information about an existing feature or service.
- **Service Fulfillment request**. This is a request to gain access to a feature or service offered through the IT Service Catalog.
- **New Service request**. This is a request to provide a new feature or service.
- **Incident Resolution request**. This is a request to resolve the failure of a service or component to provide a feature that it was designed to deliver.

After categorization and prioritization of the user's request is completed, the CSR should be prepared to resolve the user's request.

Process 3a: Resolve an Information Request

Among the activities involved in resolving an Information request include:

- Searching for and locating applicable knowledge base articles.
- Determining if the articles are user-ready and sending them to the user, if appropriate.
- Verifying the successful receipt of the articles and assisting the user with the application of the knowledge, if necessary.
- Updating the Help request with the knowledge base articles that were shared with the user.

Process 3b: Resolve a Request for an Existing Feature or Service

If the CSR determines that the user has a Service Fulfillment request, this portion of the flow guides the CSR to locate the appropriate directions and satisfy the user's needs.

The activities involved in resolving a request for an existing feature or service include:

- Searching for and locating the correct service fulfillment procedure.
- Initiating the fulfillment procedure.

Process 3c: Resolve a Request for a New Feature or Service
Resolving a request for a feature or service that is not included in the IT Service Catalog involves:
- Filtering the new service request to determine whether it should be accepted or rejected.
- Deciding whether to handle the request as a standard change New Service request.
- Deciding whether to handle the request as a non-standard change New Service request.

Process 3d: Resolve an Incident Resolution Request
Incident resolution is a process that is specifically focused on rapidly restoring a service to a state from which it can fulfill its documented goals. The resolution can involve a single step or multiple steps, as the example in the following figure illustrates.

The process flow for incident resolution consists of the following processes:
- Troubleshooting the incident
- Escalating, if necessary
- Applying a fix or workaround

Process 4: Confirm Resolution and Close the Request
After the Help request has been fulfilled, you must confirm that the Help request has been resolved and then close the request in this process.

The activities involved in confirming resolution and closing the request include:

- Updating the Help request.
- Determining if the service has been resumed.
- Determining if the incident has been resolved.
- Verifying successful fulfillment.
- Closing the Help request.

Process 5: Ensure Good Service

The final process in customer service is ensuring that the Service Desk has provided good service to the user. This is done through Service Desk quality assurance and SLA monitoring and metrics.

Process 5a: Service Desk Quality Assurance

Service Desk quality assurance is an extremely important part of ensuring good service. Good customer feedback can help to justify continued Service Desk staffing and funding, as well as help with the continuous improvement of the customer service process.

The activities involved in Service Desk quality assurance include:
- Verifying the resolution of the Help request.
- Sending a user satisfaction survey.

Process 5b: SLA Monitoring and Metrics

Although SLAs have traditionally focused on measuring technical services, it is important that support services also be measured and monitored. Help request volumes can be significant and IT operations managers cannot manually monitor queues and select incidents that need additional attention. SLA monitoring for Support Services takes over this task.

The activities involved in SLA monitoring and metrics include:
- Determining if the SLA is 80 percent expired.
- Alerting the Help request owner.
- Alerting management staff and the business.

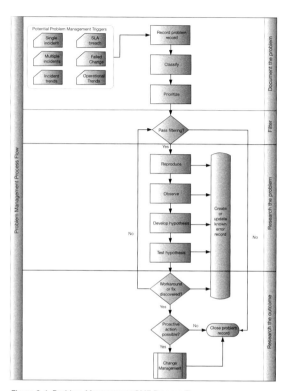

Figure 6-4. Problem Management SMF Process Flow

Problem Management SMF

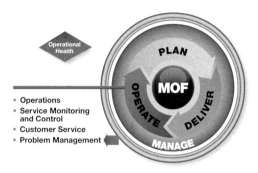

- Operations
- Service Monitoring and Control
- Customer Service
- Problem Management

Why Use the Problem Management SMF?

This SMF should be useful to anyone who is tasked with identifying underlying problems to prevent incidents before they occur. Typically, the focus of Problem Management is on complex problems that are beyond the scope of a request for incident resolution.

Specifically, this SMF addresses how to:

- Document the problem.
- Filter the problem.
- Research the problem.
- Research the outcome.

Goals of Problem Management

The primary goal of Problem Management is to reduce the occurrence of failures with IT services. Its secondary goals are to generate data and lessons that IT can use to provide feedback during the IT lifecycle and to help drive the development of more stable solutions.

Table 6-7. Outcomes and Measures of the Problem Management SMF Goals

Outcomes	Measures
Problems affecting infrastructure and service are identified and assigned an owner.	• The number of unassigned problems is reduced, and the number of problems assigned to an owner is increased.
Steps are identified and taken to reduce the impact of incidents and problems.	• The number of incidents and problems that occur is reduced, and the impact of those that still occur is lessened.
Root cause is identified for problems, and activity is initiated to establish workarounds or permanent solutions to identified problems.	• The number of workarounds and permanent solutions to identified problems is increased.
Trend analysis is used to predict future problems and enable prioritization of problems.	• More problems are resolved earlier or avoided entirely.

Problem Management Processes and Activities

Process 1: Document the Problem

The first process in Problem Management is to thoroughly document the problem. This includes classifying and prioritizing the problem.

A problem is any scenario that threatens the reliability or availability of a service or system. Problems may arise from many sources and can be triggered by many events. For a problem to qualify for Problem Management, however, there must be value in documenting the problem by doing research on it and attempting to locate and resolve its root cause. In addition, the value of removing the problem from the environment should be greater than the effort and cost to do so.

Record keeping is critical to Problem Management. If the problem's data is lost, duplicated, or incorrectly recorded, Problem Management cannot function correctly. The success of the process depends on having good data to analyze and research.

Note: It is important to remember that if a service or system is interrupted, this is considered an incident and not a problem. Be very careful not to get in the way of the service resumption activity of incident resolution, which is described in the *Customer Service SMF*.

The activities involved in documenting a problem include:

- Creating a problem record.
- Prioritizing the problem.
- Classifying the problem.

Process 2: Filter the Problem

During this process, you filter the problem to decide whether to pursue solving it.

Process 3: Research the Problem

After making the decision to solve the problem, the next process is to do research to find a fix.

For effective and meaningful Problem Management, researching a problem must follow disciplines similar to those of the scientific method. This includes:

- Reproducing the problem in a test environment.
- Observing the symptoms of the problem and noting your observations.
- Performing root cause analysis.
- Developing a hypothesis and testing it.
- Repeating this process until the root cause has been determined.

At first glance, this may seem overly complicated. But, it is critical that Problem Management identifies the root cause of the problem and determines the steps to eliminate it. This process allows you to examine one variable at a time. This is important because introducing multiple variables all at once can make it impossible to isolate the valuable ones. This could lead to deploying ineffective or over-complicated fixes.

The output of this process is the production of a known error record. However, since it can be difficult to pinpoint exactly when the data required to create the known error record will become apparent, you should ask the following questions during each activity in this process. If the answer to any of the questions is yes, it's time to create the known error record:

- Has information been discovered that would aid others in resolving incidents or events matching the specific problem?
- Has a definitive root cause been identified?
- Have any actions been uncovered that would reduce the frequency or impact of the error?
- Can a date be projected for when the error will be resolved?
- Is there meaningful information available to share about the progress of resolving the error?
- Are there actions that Problem Management needs individuals to take to aid in the research efforts?
- Has a workaround been discovered?
- Has a fix been designed?

This process has the following activities:

- Reproducing the problem.
- Observing the symptoms of the problem.
- Performing root cause analysis.
- Developing a hypothesis.
- Testing the hypothesis.

Root Cause Analysis Techniques

A difficult area of Problem Management for most organizations is analyzing the root cause of a problem. Root cause analysis techniques are used to identify the conditions that initiate an undesired activity or state. Since problems are best solved by attempting to correct or eliminate their root causes, this is a critical part of resolving any problem.

There are many techniques available for performing root cause analysis. Two of the most popular are:

- Fishbone diagrams.
- Fault tree analysis.

Process 4: Research the Outcome

Once the first pass through the research process has been completed, it is time to look at the results and determine if a viable workaround or fix has been discovered. Because of the complex nature of IT and the intricacies of highly integrated systems, you might need to perform the research process a number of times in order to achieve a workaround or fix.

If you repeat the research process, you must go through the filtering activity each time. This gives you the opportunity to re-evaluate the value of continuing the effort to resolve the problem. If the resolution to the problem becomes too difficult to find, it might be time to stop your attempts and focus on a more achievable goal.

The activities involved in researching the outcome include:

- Determining if a workaround or fix has been discovered.
- Determining if a proactive action is possible.
- Closing the problem record.

Proactive Analysis

Proactive analysis activities are concerned with identifying and resolving problems before they occur, thereby minimizing their adverse impact on the service and business as a whole. This can be accomplished by reviewing:

- The current problem record database.
- All escalated events stored in an incident tracking system.
- Corporate error report data.
- Knowledge base articles containing "unknown error" state.

Selecting which problems to attempt to resolve proactively should be based on a number of factors, including:

- The cost to the business.
- The customers affected.
- The volume, duration, and cost of the problems.
- The cost of implementation.
- The likelihood of success.

Using these factors, an algorithm can be created and used to calculate the business impact of support events. This can be a useful, cost-effective way to determine which problems to address.

Improving Operations in Your Organization

Use the following checklist to determine the right set of priorities for your organization. To support the right set of decisions, refer to the MOF guidance, which provides key questions, inputs, outputs and best practices that support decision making: www.microsoft.com/mof.

Operations SMF Checklist

- Define operational requirements.
- Build operational work instructions.
- Plan operational work.
- Execute operational work.
- Maintain operational work instructions.
- Manage operational work.

Key Questions

- Have you made an operations plan that details the operational requirements, activities, and tasks, including the requirements and dependencies?
- Have you developed proper guidance and specific Instructions for the operational work identified in the operations plan?
- Have you properly assigned the resources, identified the dependencies and estimated the duration for the operational work?
- Have you put plans in place so that you can continually improve the quality of service delivery based on the knowledge gathered while performing the operational work?
- Have better ways of completing work been identified? Are they thorough enough that existing work instructions can be retired?
- Is work outlined in the operations guide being done cost-effectively and within the parameters of the SLA?

Service Monitoring and Control SMF Checklist

- Define SMC requirements
- Implement Service
- Continuous monitoring
- Control and reporting

Key Questions

- Do you have the proper information and data needed to make a health model?
- Is the new service aligned well with existing IT processes and functions?
- Do you have a smooth continuous monitoring procedure in place?
- Are you generating information for the entire IT organization and ensuring that monitoring is constantly performed?

Customer Service SMF Checklist

- Record the user's request.
- Classify the user's request.
- Resolve the request.
- Confirm resolution and close the request.
- Ensure good service.

Key Questions

- Do you have procedures in place that will ensure the CSR takes the proper information from a user?
- Do you have the proper information and guidance in place to make sure the CSR categorizes the request properly?
- Do the CSRs have proper guidance on how to properly categorize each request for easy resolution?
- Was the request addressed successfully, and is there a way to further improve the procedure?

- Are there proper procedures in place to monitor Service Desk quality assurance as well as SLA monitoring and metrics?

Problem Management SMF Checklist

- Document the problem.
- Filter the problem.
- Research the problem.
- Research the outcome.

Key Questions

- Do you have proper procedures in place for record keeping and ensuring that good data is recorded for analysis and research?
- Does removing the problem offer more value than the effort and cost to do so?
- Can you reproduce the problem in a test environment?
- Upon doing your research, have you been able to determine a workaround or fix for the problem?

7. Getting Started with MOF 4.0: Microsoft© Products and Solutions

Microsoft's© core service management strategy is to deliver solutions for the effective and efficient integration of the people, process, and technologies required for organizations to reap the benefits of quality IT services. As shown in the following figure, Microsoft© provides people and process guidance with MOF 4.0, management tools with the System Center family of products, and integrated technology and guidance packages to handle complex problems with Solution Accelerators. When combined, MOF 4.0, Solution Accelerators, and System Center products support optimized service delivery and management of the Windows operating system platform—which in turn delivers the core IT infrastructure required to support business services and workloads.

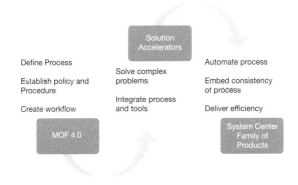

Solution Accelerators

Define Process

Establish policy and Procedure

Create workflow

MOF 4.0

Solve complex problems

Integrate process and tools

Automate process

Embed consistency of process

Deliver efficiency

System Center Family of Products

Figure 7-1. The Microsoft© Windows Platform

System Center Family of Products

To increase an organization's service management capability requires the integration and automation of process and IT pro activities. The Microsoft© System Center family of products facilitates this automation and integration, helping to reduce service management complexity and delivering a reliable and consistent operations experience designed especially for the Microsoft© environment including Windows Server, Microsoft© SQL Server, Microsoft© Exchange, the Microsof©t Office System, and the Microsoft©.Net Framework. Automation of the service management frameworks is achieved via three key features of the System Center products:

- **Embedded knowledge**. Infrastructure data is captured and used intelligently in order to help automate the service management processes.
- **Integration**. All System Center products work tightly together to present the IT professional with a consistent technology architecture that allows for workflows across the different products.
- **Flexibility**. System Center provides customizable models and process templates as well as the ability to work with different technologies.

The System Center family of products includes the following:

- **System Center Operations Manager 2007**. Providing service monitoring of distributed applications, Operations Manager 2007 enables IT staff to have greater control of the IT environment.
- **System Center Configuration Manager 2007**. Enabling greater control over desktop and servers, Configuration Manager provides tools for managing desired system configurations including automating software installations and updates.

- **System Center Data Protection Manager 2006**. Delivering continuous data protection for Windows file servers, Data Protection Manager provides backup and restore capabilities.
- **System Center Essentials 2007**. To enable IT staff in smaller organizations to manage their environments more effectively, Essentials provides a tool that unifies two of the most important management functions: monitoring distributed systems and automating software installation.
- **System Center Virtual Machine Manager**. A new kind of management tool for the new age of virtualization, this product helps management staff with consolidating applications onto virtualized servers.
- **System Center Service Manager**, scheduled for release in 2010, will provide comprehensive, easy to use, and customizable Service Desk capabilities, a central integration point for service management workflows across the System Center family of products, and built-in support for service management best practice frameworks like MOF and ITIL®. Service Manager will differentiate itself by:
  - Enabling integration across System Center solutions and other common industry management tools
  - Delivering core Service Desk functionality with workflows integrated across System Center solutions
  - Making customization a straightforward process without challenges in future versions or updates
  - Providing an easy to use and intuitive experience for all user types

For more information on Service Manager, including current release timelines and opportunities for early adoption, visit the Service Manager website at www.microsoft.com/systemcenter/svcmgr/default.mspx, and the System Center blog at blogs.technet.com/systemcenter.

For more information on the System Center Family of products, visit:

- System Center Configuration Manager www.microsoft.com/systemcenter/configmgr/default.mspx
- System Center Operations Manager www.microsoft.com/systemcenter/opsmgr/default.mspx
- System Center Data Protection Manager www.microsoft.com/systemcenter/dpm/default.mspx
- System Center Virtual Machine Manager www.microsoft.com/systemcenter/scvmm/default.mspx
- System Center Essentials www.microsoft.com/systemcenter/essentials/default.mspx
- System Center Mobile Device Manager 2008 www.microsoft.com/systemcenter/mobile/default.mspx
- System Center Capacity Planner 2007 www.microsoft.com/systemcenter/sccp/default.mspx

Solution Accelerators

Solution Accelerators integrate System Center technologies with integrated MOF guidance to deliver packaged solutions to the complex problems of IT service delivery. Solution Accelerators cover many areas of the IT infrastructure, including:

- Desktop, Device and Server Management
- Automated Assessments
- Communication and Collaboration
- Security Process and Compliance
- Content Management
- Data Protection and Recovery
- Identity and Access Management
- IT Process and Frameworks

For example, the Solution Accelerator for Business Desktop Deployment (BDD) is best-practice guidance for desktop deployment, aimed at reducing deployment time, effort, and cost by increasing the level of automation. It allows administrators to deploy desktops with Zero Touch and Lite Touch interaction at the target PCs. This solution also helps organizations move to a managed environment with standardized desktop images, thereby reducing system complexity and increasing its overall manageability. BDD uses System Center technologies to automate the software distribution process and works with the underpinning of the core Windows infrastructure to make it possible.

Delivering IT Service Management: Getting Started with Tangible Assets from Microsoft©

Where to begin on the journey to delivering service management depends on where you are and what your current and most relevant challenges are. For example:

- If you want to understand where your organization is with respect to its ability to implement the IT service lifecycle and achieve dynamic systems, you can learn more about the Infrastructure Optimization (IO) model at technet.microsoft.com/en-us/ infrastructure/default.aspx and then assess yourself. This will give you a better idea of where your IT infrastructure is and how you can improve on it.

- If you want to automate your service management processes and would like to know more about available tools to make it happen, visit www.microsoft.com/systemcenter/default.aspx.

- If you already have an idea of where your problems are with respect to service management, you would greatly benefit from looking at the different Solution Accelerators at www.microsoft. com/technet/solutionaccelerators/default.mspx and identifying those that you might be able to implement in order to optimize your current IT infrastructure.

- If you need help in identifying or further qualifying the problems that you may have in service management, then doing a Service Management Assessment of your organization would be the best step to take to ensure that resources are allocated to the right problems. Contact your technical account manager or account representative at www.microsoft.com/services/microsoftservices/default.mspx to learn how.
- Finally, if you would like to learn more about the Microsoft© strategy for IT service lifecycle management, visit the MOF 4.0 website at www.microsoft.com/mof.